THE "I LOVE MY AIR FRYER"

Comfort Food

RECIPE BOOK

From *Chicken Parmesan* to *Small Batch Chocolate Chip Cookies*,
175 Easy and Delicious Recipes

Aileen Clark of AileenCooks.com
Author of *The "I Love My Air Fryer"
Affordable Meals Recipe Book*

Adams Media

New York   London   Toronto   Sydney   New Delhi

Aadamsmedia

Adams Media
An Imprint of Simon & Schuster, Inc.
100 Technology Center Drive
Stoughton, Massachusetts 02072

First Adams Media trade paperback edition August 2023

ADAMS MEDIA and colophon are registered trademarks of Simon & Schuster, Inc.

For information about special discounts for bulk purchases, please contact Simon & Schuster Special Sales at 1-866-506-1949 or business@simonandschuster.com.

The Simon & Schuster Speakers Bureau can bring authors to your live event. For more information or to book an event, contact the Simon & Schuster Speakers Bureau at 1-866-248-3049 or visit our website at www.simonspeakers.com.

Photographs by James Stefiuk

Manufactured in the United States of America

1 2023

Library of Congress Cataloging-in-Publication Data
Names: Clark, Aileen, author.
Title: The "I love my air fryer" comfort food recipe book / Aileen Clark of AileenCooks.com, author of The "I love my air fryer" affordable meals recipe book.
Description: First Adams Media trade paperback edition. | Stoughton, Massachusetts: Adams Media, 2023. | Series: "I love my" cookbook series | Includes index.
Identifiers: LCCN 2023005837 | ISBN 9781507220375 (pb) | ISBN 9781507220382 (ebook)
Subjects: LCSH: Hot air frying. | Comfort food. | LCGFT: Cookbooks.
Classification: LCC TX689 .C59 2023 | DDC 641.7/7--dc23/eng/20230301
LC record available at https://lccn.loc.gov/2023005837

ISBN 978-1-5072-2037-5
ISBN 978-1-5072-2038-2 (ebook)

Contents

Introduction

Remember the mouthwatering taste of a rib eye steak followed by a piece of warm apple pie from a special family dinner? Or the delicious smell of egg rolls and sweet and sour chicken from your favorite Chinese restaurant? These special foods are your "comfort foods"—foods that make you feel good whether it's because of sentimental attachment or the food's texture, flavor, or even temperature. Good news! The pleasure of your comfort foods is closer and easier than you think. With the air fryer you can quickly and easily cook healthier versions of your favorite comfort foods in your own home—without sacrificing flavor or your wallet.

The air fryer is an amazing appliance that can take the place of many appliances and gadgets traditionally needed to make great-tasting meals, such as the oven, dehydrator, microwave, deep fryer, and more. Not only that, but the air fryer does its cooking in less time than traditional methods. The versatility of the air fryer allows you to make breakfasts, decadent desserts, side dishes, and dinners too. As an added benefit, this machine makes foods taste great without the huge amounts of oil that traditional deep fryers use, making it a healthier alternative to the particular comfort foods that are traditionally deep-fried.

Whether you're an experienced air fryer user or someone just looking for their first appliance, you'll find information in Chapter 1 that ensures your comfort dishes taste great! Regardless of your skill level with the air fryer, this chapter can act as a refresher or go-to guide in the kitchen. Here you will learn how to make new and exciting dishes in your air fryer along with how to choose the best air fryer for your family, which accessories to invest in, and how to deal with cook time variations with your ingredients.

Everyone has a comfort food that is special to them. The "I Love My Air Fryer" Comfort Food Recipe Book includes 175 recipes perfect for anyone's special dish, whether you like warm, hearty meals like steak, potatoes, and casseroles, or sweet snack foods like muffins, pies, and cookies. For breakfast, serve your family and friends some hearty Cheesy Breakfast Potatoes or Biscuits and Gravy Casserole. Want a snack? Try some Queso Dip or Bunless Burger Bites. If you need a full meal, sample the Salsa Chicken Casserole, Sweet and Sour Pork, Coconut Curry Salmon, or Chickpea No-Meat Balls. Or, if you have a sweet tooth, try the Chewy Chocolate Chip Brownies, rich S'mores, or traditional Monkey Bread. Whatever recipe you choose, know you will end up with a delicious, quick, and healthier alternative to the way your parent or guardian made it.

The "I Love My Air Fryer" Comfort Food Recipe Book will be the only resource you need to make your air fryer your new favorite kitchen appliance. Personalize your favorite comfort foods and make new memories. Bring out your air fryer and get cooking!

Cooking with an Air Fryer

Cooking with an air fryer may seem daunting at first, but it is actually incredibly easy! Not only does it make tasty fried foods without all of the oil, but it can also cook everything from breakfast to dessert in little time. Food cooked in an air fryer comes out tasting amazing because the air fryer technology adds an extra crispness that you used to only be able to get with a deep fryer. The extra crispiness is great for recipes that used to require the deep fryer, and adds a great new texture to baked goods that will enhance the flavor.

In this chapter, you will learn the basics of cooking with an air fryer, how to choose an air fryer, and how to learn to use your particular model. You will also get helpful tips on efficiently re-creating the delicious tastes of your childhood comfort foods—and they will be healthier without the excess oil.

Why Air Frying?

Air fryers are a great alternative to deep-frying food. It is a healthier option and makes foods come out crispier than they would in the microwave or even in the oven. Air fryers not only make traditional deep-fried foods, but can cook chicken and steak, childhood favorites like mac and cheese, vegetables, breakfast items such as bacon, and lots of fun desserts like cookies and brownies.

Depending on the type of air fryer you choose, they can take up very little space in your kitchen. Air fryers also don't heat up your kitchen the way a traditional oven does. These machines are a great way to cook in the summer without adding extra heat to your home. Air fryers also tend to cook things quite quickly. Many recipes take 30 minutes or less to cook, and several take 10 minutes or less. This is very different from traditional comfort food that can take close to an hour, or hours, to prep and bake!

Choosing an Air Fryer

There are two different types of air fryers (and many, many different brands). The two main types of air fryers are basket-style and oven-style. Either is a great option, and the type you buy depends on your personal preferences. Either type of air fryer can be used when making the recipes in this cookbook.

- **Basket-style air fryers**, as their name implies, are air fryers where food is cooked in a removable basket. These air fryers take up less space in your kitchen and can be easier to clean than their counterparts.

- **Oven-style air fryers** tend to have extra options, like rotisserie, room for baking sheets, and multiple racks. Some air fryer ovens even offer the option to defrost or slow cook but are more difficult to clean. Oven-style air fryers also hold more food, making it less likely that you will need to cook recipes in batches, as you may need to with a basket-style air fryer. Of course, adding options and room to cook does make them much larger than a standard basket-style air fryer.

Another thing to look for when purchasing an air fryer is the capacity inside the air fryer. You should look for one that is at least 5 quarts. Even if only cooking for one or two people, you will run into occasions when you want enough room in your machine to cook more than one serving and the food you are cooking may not fit inside a smaller air fryer.

Also, many air fryers offer additional capabilities. Many air fryers work as dehydrators, roasters, and rotisseries too. Make a list of the capabilities you want before shopping for an air fryer so you can ensure you get the one with all of the bells and whistles you prefer.

Air Fryer Accessories

You don't need a lot of accessories for your air fryer, as it has many functions on its own, but there are a few accessories we use in this book.

- **Small Cake Pan:** This pan is used for cakes, quiche, and casseroles. The cake pan used in this cookbook is a 7" aluminum cake pan. Make sure the pan you get fits inside your chosen air fryer.

- **Silicone Egg Mold:** This mold is perfect for eggs and muffins.
- **Small Bundt Pan:** Bundt pans make recipes look pretty and are great for making pull-apart recipes like pizza bread and monkey bread.
- **Tongs:** Tongs are also a great tool to have on hand for flipping foods over and removing them from your air fryer.
- **Parchment Paper:** This is an essential kitchen tool that will help prep food before, during, and after air frying.
- **Meat Thermometer:** Cooking meat safely is incredibly important. You will need to use this thermometer for any meat-based dish you make.
- **Plastic Spatula:** A plastic or silicone spatula is important for flipping foods in the air fryer. Metal spatulas can scrape off the nonstick coating, so it's important not to use metal.
- **Skewers:** Metal or wooden skewers can be used in the air fryer. It is important to soak wooden skewers in water prior to air frying.

Safe Removal of Accessories

When removing accessories and food from an air fryer, you should treat it just like an oven. Everything inside the air fryer gets very hot and will burn you if you are not careful. Make sure to take extra precautions by always using oven mitts when removing food and accessories from your air fryer.

Operating Your Air Fryer Safely

Each air fryer is different and must be operated carefully. Many models will have differences in cook times and may or may not preheat. To keep things safe and functional, stay away from nonstick sprays, and be sure to clean your machine regularly following the instructions in the user manual or in this section.

Cook Time Variations

As there are many different variations of air fryers, there are cook time variations depending on the style and size of your air fryer too. Whenever trying a new recipe, keep an eye on your food, as it may need to be taken out of the air fryer a couple of minutes early or air fried for a couple of extra minutes. This is normal. As you get used to your air fryer, you will learn how quickly it cooks. It also helps to add a note in the cookbook if you ended up needing to change the air fry time. The air fryer used in this cookbook is a basket-style air fryer with a capacity of 5.8 quarts.

Preheating an Air Fryer

All of the recipes in this cookbook require the air fryer to be preheated prior to cooking. This ensures consistency throughout all recipes and helps keep the cooking times accurate. Refer to your air fryer owner's manual on directions for preheating your air fryer.

Using Cooking Spray

In this cookbook, you will see that only olive oil spray is recommended to spray inside of your air fryer. Standard nonstick sprays contain additional chemicals that can wear down the coating in your air fryer. Make sure to read the ingredients when

purchasing the olive oil spray to ensure it contains only oil.

Cleaning Your Air Fryer

It's important to clean your air fryer after each use. Don't wait to clean your air fryer, or the food will get caked on and will be much harder to wash. Before you wash the air fryer, please make sure it is cool to the touch and unplugged. Start by washing your air fryer basket or trays with warm soapy water. Use a toothpick or other small sharp tool to clean out any food stuck in the air holes. Wipe the inside of the air fryer with a damp towel. Finally, wipe the outside of the air fryer with a damp towel.

2

Breakfast

Looking to start your day on a delicious note? Good news: There are many comfort food breakfast items that can be made in the air fryer! These breakfasts are perfect for those slower mornings when you can take your time making something tasty. The air fryer cuts your cook time down and allows your favorite dishes to bake, cook, or fry to perfection. If you are in the mood for something sweet, start your morning with the delicious Triple-Berry Breakfast Tarts, a Cinnamon Streusel Coffee Cake, or some Double Chocolate Muffins. Savory more your style? Try a breakfast of Sausage and Cheddar Egg Muffins, pair some Scotch Eggs with Bacon Crescent Rolls, or have a serving of Biscuits and Gravy Casserole. Regardless of your preferences, you are sure to start off on the right foot with any of these mouthwatering recipes.

Everything Bagels

Ever wanted to make your own bagels? This surefire recipe produces bagels with the perfect texture from the air fryer. These homemade bagels require only four ingredients. Step up your breakfast game by making a batch for your family! The recipe is extremely versatile: It can be made without the everything seasoning if you like a plain bagel; can be served with cream cheese, butter, avocado, or peanut butter; or can be made into a ham and cheese sandwich.

Hands-On Time: 15 minutes
Cook Time: 12 minutes (per batch)

Makes 5

1 cup self-rising flour plus more for rolling
1 cup plain Greek yogurt
2 tablespoons salted butter, melted
2 tablespoons everything bagel seasoning

EVERYTHING IN EVERYTHING BAGEL SEASONING

Everything bagel seasoning is a simple seasoning mix made of just six ingredients. It can be purchased in the spice aisle of your local grocery store, or it can be made by combining 2 teaspoons sesame seeds, 1½ teaspoons black sesame seeds, 1½ teaspoons minced dried garlic, 1½ teaspoons minced dried onion, ½ teaspoon poppy seeds, and 1 teaspoon salt.

1 Preheat air fryer to 350°F.

2 In a large bowl, combine 1 cup flour and Greek yogurt. Mix until a sticky dough forms. Pour dough onto a well-floured surface. Divide dough into five equal pieces and shape them into bagels.

3 Spray inside of air fryer with olive oil spray before each batch. Arrange bagels inside air fryer, spaced ½" apart (you may need to work in batches). Air fry 12 minutes.

4 Remove bagels from air fryer. Brush tops of bagels with melted butter and sprinkle with everything bagel seasoning. Transfer bagels to a wire cooling rack. Let cool 10 minutes and serve.

PER SERVING

CALORIES: 197 | FAT: 7g | SODIUM: 734mg | CARBOHYDRATES: 20g | FIBER: 1g | SUGAR: 2g | PROTEIN: 7g

Chocolate Chip Scones

Using frozen, grated butter for the recipe makes for a lighter scone, as it allows the butter to melt in the oven, not during prep. Use mini chocolate chips in this recipe, as they distribute evenly through the batter. These scones can be stored at room temperature in an airtight container for 2 days or in the refrigerator for 1 week.

Hands-On Time: 30 minutes
Cook Time: 6 minutes (per batch)

Serves 8

- 2¼ cups all-purpose flour, divided
- 2½ teaspoons baking powder
- 1 teaspoon ground cinnamon
- ½ teaspoon salt
- ½ cup unsalted butter, frozen and grated
- ½ cup heavy whipping cream
- ½ cup packed light brown sugar
- 1 large egg
- 1½ teaspoons vanilla extract
- ¾ cup semisweet mini chocolate chips
- 2 tablespoons granulated sugar
- ¼ cup confectioners' sugar

1 Preheat air fryer to 360°F.

2 In a large bowl, whisk together 2 cups flour, baking powder, cinnamon, and salt until combined. Add grated butter into flour mixture and mix together with two forks or a pastry cutter until dough is crumbly with pea-sized crumbs. Place mixture in the refrigerator 10 minutes.

3 In a medium bowl, mix together whipping cream, brown sugar, egg, and vanilla.

4 Remove flour mixture from refrigerator. Mix wet ingredients into dry ingredients until mixture is moistened. Fold in mini chocolate chips. The dough will be tough.

5 Sprinkle remaining ¼ cup flour onto a clean surface and place dough onto flour. Knead dough two to three times until no longer sticky, then form dough into a ball. Roll dough out to a 12" circle, about ½" thick. Use a pizza cutter or sharp knife to cut the circle into eight equal triangular pieces.

6 Spray inside of air fryer with olive oil spray before each batch. Working in batches, arrange scones inside air fryer, spaced ½" apart, and sprinkle with granulated sugar. Air fry 6 minutes or until golden brown on top.

7 Remove from air fryer and sprinkle with confectioners' sugar. Let cool 10 minutes. Serve.

PER SERVING

CALORIES: 459 | FAT: 21g | SODIUM: 319mg | CARBOHYDRATES: 61g | FIBER: 2g | SUGAR: 32g | PROTEIN: 6g

Lemon-Glazed Blueberry Scones

These delicate, fruity scones are like sunshine wrapped up in a pastry. They can be stored at room temperature in an airtight container for 2 days or in the refrigerator for 1 week.

Hands-On Time: 30 minutes
Cook Time: 6 minutes (per batch)

Serves 8

Scones
2¼ cups all-purpose flour, divided
2½ teaspoons baking powder
½ teaspoon salt
½ cup unsalted butter, frozen and grated
½ cup heavy whipping cream
½ cup packed light brown sugar
1 large egg
1½ teaspoons vanilla extract
1 cup blueberries
2 tablespoons granulated sugar

Glaze
½ cup lemon juice
1 tablespoon unsalted butter, melted
2 cups confectioners' sugar, sifted
1 tablespoon lemon zest

HISTORY OF SCONES
Scones originated in Scotland back in the 1500s. They were originally made with oats but have since evolved to be made from flour like the recipes in this chapter.

1 To make scones: Preheat air fryer to 360°F.

2 In a large bowl, whisk together 2 cups flour, baking powder, and salt until combined. Add grated butter into flour mixture and mix together with two forks or a pastry cutter until dough is crumbly with pea-sized crumbs. Place mixture in the refrigerator for 10 minutes.

3 In a medium bowl, mix together whipping cream, brown sugar, egg, and vanilla.

4 Remove flour mixture from refrigerator. Mix wet ingredients into dry ingredients until mixture is moistened. Fold in blueberries. The dough will be tough.

5 Sprinkle remaining ¼ cup flour onto a clean surface and place dough onto flour. Knead dough two to three times until no longer sticky, then form dough into a ball. Roll dough out to a 12" circle, about ½" thick. Use a pizza cutter or sharp knife to cut the circle into eight equal triangular pieces.

6 Spray inside of air fryer with olive oil spray before each batch. Working in batches, arrange scones inside air fryer, spaced ½" apart, and sprinkle with granulated sugar. Air fry 6 minutes or until golden brown on top.

7 To make glaze: Whisk together lemon juice, melted butter, confectioners' sugar, and zest. Continue to mix until sugar is dissolved.

8 Remove from air fryer and let cool 10 minutes. Drizzle glaze over scones. Serve.

PER SERVING

CALORIES: 480 | FAT: 18g | SODIUM: 318mg | CARBOHYDRATES: 73g | FIBER: 2g | SUGAR: 44g | PROTEIN: 5g

Triple-Berry Breakfast Tarts

These tarts taste great fresh from the air fryer or cooled to room temperature. You can reheat them in the air fryer or toast them in your toaster (without the berry compote). They can be stored at room temperature in an airtight container for 2 days or frozen up to 3 months.

Hands-On Time: 20 minutes
Cook Time: 12 minutes

Serves 4

½ cup blueberries
½ cup hulled and sliced strawberries
½ cup raspberries
¼ cup granulated sugar
2 teaspoons cornstarch, divided
½ (15-ounce) package refrigerated premade pie crust dough (1 pie crust)
1 large egg
1 tablespoon water
½ cup confectioners' sugar
1 tablespoon lemon juice

FROZEN BERRY SUBSTITUTE

If you're making these tarts outside of berry season, a bag of frozen mixed berries may be used. A single type of frozen berry will also work, though you will not get the variety of flavor. Simply measure out 1½ cups berries and allow them to thaw prior to cooking.

1 Heat a medium saucepan over medium-high heat. Combine berries and granulated sugar in the saucepan, then mash using a potato masher. Bring to a boil, stirring constantly, about 5 minutes. Mix in 1 teaspoon cornstarch and let boil 1 minute. Remove from heat and let cool 3 minutes.

2 Preheat air fryer to 370°F.

3 Unroll pie crust and shape into a rectangle using your fingers. Cut the pie crust vertically into four equal pieces. Cut each piece in half. Place a scoop of berry mixture in the centers of half of the crust pieces and spread it, reserving the leftover berry sauce. Place remaining crusts on top of fruit-filled ones. Press edges together.

4 In a small bowl, whisk together egg and water. Brush on top of each tart.

5 Spray inside of air fryer with olive oil spray. Arrange tarts inside air fryer, spaced ½" apart. Air fry 6 minutes or until golden brown around the edges.

6 Combine berry sauce, confectioners' sugar, and lemon juice and whisk until smooth. Mix in remaining 1 teaspoon cornstarch and whisk again.

7 Remove tarts from air fryer and let cool 10 minutes. Drizzle tarts with berry sauce before serving.

PER SERVING

CALORIES: 381 | FAT: 14g | SODIUM: 235mg | CARBOHYDRATES: 60g | FIBER: 3g | SUGAR: 28g | PROTEIN: 4g

Chocolate and Peanut Butter Breakfast Tarts

These yummy breakfast tarts are made with a flaky, buttery pie crust, which stays relatively thin, so they can be reheated in the toaster. The combination of chocolate hazelnut spread and creamy peanut butter tastes great while offering a bit of protein to your morning meal. If you don't have creamy peanut butter on hand, crunchy peanut butter may be substituted.

Hands-On Time: 15 minutes
Cook Time: 10 minutes

Serves 4

½ (15-ounce) package refrigerated premade pie crust dough (1 pie crust)
¾ cup chocolate hazelnut spread
¾ cup creamy peanut butter
1 large egg
1 tablespoon water
¼ cup white candy melts
¼ cup light cocoa melts
2 tablespoons chocolate sprinkles

1 Preheat air fryer to 370°F.

2 Unroll pie crust and gently shape into a rectangle using your fingers or a rolling pin. Cut the pie crust vertically into four equal pieces. Cut each piece in half. Spoon 2 tablespoons chocolate hazelnut spread and 2 tablespoons peanut butter into the center of half of the pie crust pieces. Place remaining pie crust pieces on top of filled ones. Press edges together with the tines of a fork.

3 In a small bowl, whisk together egg and water to make an egg wash. Brush egg wash on top of each tart.

4 Spray inside of air fryer with olive oil spray. Arrange tarts inside air fryer, spaced ½" apart. Air fry 6 minutes or until golden brown around the edges. Make sure to check tarts often, as they can burn quickly. Remove from air fryer and let cool 5 minutes.

5 Place candy and cocoa melts in two small microwave-safe bowls. Melt according to package instructions, about 4 minutes total.

6 Spread white melts over tarts. Then drizzle tarts with light cocoa melts. Top with sprinkles and let cool an additional 5 minutes before serving.

PER SERVING

CALORIES: 840 | **FAT:** 50g | **SODIUM:** 414mg | **CARBOHYDRATES:** 83g | **FIBER:** 4g | **SUGAR:** 48g | **PROTEIN:** 15g

Cheese Danish

These classic Cheese Danish feature a creamy cheese center on flaky puff pastry topped with a delicious glaze. The cheese filling is made with cream cheese, confectioners' sugar, vanilla, lemon juice, and an egg yolk.

Hands-On Time: 20 minutes
Cook Time: 10 minutes (per batch)

Serves 8

- 1 (8-ounce) package cream cheese, softened
- 1 large egg yolk plus 1 large egg, divided
- 1½ cups confectioners' sugar, divided
- 1 teaspoon lemon juice
- 2 teaspoons vanilla extract, divided
- 1 (17.3-ounce) package frozen puff pastry, thawed
- 1 teaspoon water
- 1 tablespoon whole milk

1 Preheat air fryer to 380°F.

2 In a medium bowl, combine cream cheese, egg yolk, ½ cup sugar, lemon juice, and 1 teaspoon vanilla. Use an electric mixer on medium speed to mix until light and fluffy, about 1 minute.

3 Spread puff pastry sheets on a clean surface. Cut each sheet into four squares and fold each corner in by ½".

4 Spoon 2 tablespoons cream cheese in the center of each pastry square and spread with the back of a spoon over the folded-down corners (leaving ¼" around the edges).

5 In a small bowl, whisk together remaining egg and water. Brush egg wash over the exposed edges of puff pastry.

6 Spray inside of air fryer with olive oil spray before each batch. Working in batches, arrange puff pastry squares inside air fryer, spaced 1" apart. Air fry 5 minutes. Reduce heat to 320°F and air fry an additional 5 minutes.

7 Remove Danish from air fryer and allow to cool 10 minutes.

8 Whisk together remaining 1 cup sugar, remaining 1 teaspoon vanilla, and milk until a smooth glaze is formed. Drizzle over cooled Danish and serve.

PER SERVING

CALORIES: 530 | FAT: 32g | SODIUM: 267mg | CARBOHYDRATES: 48g | FIBER: 1g | SUGAR: 20g | PROTEIN: 7g

Apple Danish

To prepare your delicious Danishes ahead of time, they can be flash frozen and stored for up to 3 months. Simply arrange cooked and cooled pastries on a baking sheet so they are not touching. Freeze for 2 hours and transfer to a freezer-safe container or bag.

Hands-On Time: 20 minutes
Cook Time: 10 minutes (per batch
    plus 11 minutes on stove)

Serves 8

½ cup granulated sugar
¼ cup plus 1 teaspoon water, divided
¼ cup unsalted butter
2 teaspoons cornstarch
¾ teaspoon ground cinnamon, divided
½ teaspoon ground nutmeg
¼ teaspoon salt
2 large Granny Smith apples, peeled, cored, and diced
2 tablespoons packed light brown sugar
2 tablespoons unsalted butter, melted
¼ cup all-purpose flour
1 (17.3-ounce) package frozen puff pastry, thawed
1 large egg
1 cup confectioners' sugar
1 tablespoon whole milk
¼ teaspoon vanilla extract

1. In a saucepan over medium-high heat, combine granulated sugar, ¼ cup water, butter, cornstarch, ½ teaspoon cinnamon, nutmeg, and salt. Bring to a boil and let boil 2 minutes, stirring constantly. Mix in apples and return to a boil, mixing frequently. Cook 5 minutes or until apples are softened. Set aside.

2. In a medium bowl, mix brown sugar, remaining ¼ teaspoon cinnamon, and melted butter. Slowly mix in flour, stirring until crumbly. Set aside.

3. Preheat air fryer to 380°F. Spread puff pastry sheets on a clean surface. Cut into four squares and fold each corner in by ½". Spoon 2 tablespoons apple mixture in each pastry square and spread over the folded-down corners (leaving ¼" around the edges). Top with 1 tablespoon brown sugar mixture.

4. Whisk egg and remaining 1 teaspoon water. Brush over the exposed edges of pastry.

5. Spray inside of air fryer with olive oil spray before each batch. Working in batches, arrange puff pastry inside air fryer, spaced 1" apart. Air fry 5 minutes. Reduce heat to 320°F and air fry an additional 5 minutes.

6. Remove from air fryer and allow to cool 10 minutes.

7. Whisk together confectioners' sugar, milk, and vanilla until a smooth glaze is formed. Drizzle over cooled Danish and serve.

PER SERVING

CALORIES: 577 | FAT: 31g | SODIUM: 237mg | CARBOHYDRATES: 67g | FIBER: 2g | SUGAR: 34g | PROTEIN: 6g

Cherry Danish

These Cherry Danish taste like cherry cheesecake wrapped up in a luscious pastry. This recipe is easy to make thanks to store-bought dough and cherry pie filling, but the result yields pastries that taste just like the Danish you buy at your local bakery. Enjoy your treat on the same day or store at room temperature in an airtight container for up to 2 days.

Hands-On Time: 20 minutes
Cook Time: 10 minutes (per batch)

Serves 8

½ of 1 (8-ounce) package cream cheese, softened
1 large egg yolk plus 1 large egg, divided
¼ cup confectioners' sugar
1 teaspoon lemon juice
¼ teaspoon vanilla extract
1 (17.3-ounce) package frozen puff pastry, thawed
½ cup cherry pie filling
1 teaspoon water

1   Preheat air fryer to 380°F.

2   In a medium bowl, combine cream cheese, egg yolk, sugar, lemon juice, and vanilla. Use an electric mixer on medium speed to mix until light and fluffy, about 1 minute.

3   Spread puff pastry sheets on a clean surface. Cut each sheet into four squares and fold each corner in by ½".

4   Spoon 1 tablespoon cream cheese in the center of each puff pastry square and spread with the back of a spoon over the folded-down corners (leaving ¼" around the edges). Place 1 tablespoon cherry pie filling in the center of each pastry.

5   In a small bowl, whisk together remaining egg and water. Brush egg wash over the exposed edges of puff pastry.

6   Spray inside of air fryer with olive oil spray before each batch. Working in batches, arrange puff pastry squares inside air fryer, spaced 1" apart. Air fry 5 minutes. Reduce heat to 320°F and air fry an additional 5 minutes.

7   Remove from air fryer and let cool 10 minutes. Serve.

PER SERVING

CALORIES: 433 | **FAT:** 27g | **SODIUM:** 217mg | **CARBOHYDRATES:** 36g | **FIBER:** 1g | **SUGAR:** 4g | **PROTEIN:** 7g

Cinnamon Streusel Coffee Cake

This classic sour cream coffee cake comes out light and airy. When you make coffee cake in an air fryer, the topping is a bit crunchier than when you make it in the oven. The extra layer of texture makes the coffee cake unique.

Hands-On Time: 20 minutes
Cook Time: 15 minutes

Serves 4

Streusel
- 4 tablespoons packed light brown sugar
- ¼ teaspoon ground cinnamon
- ¼ teaspoon salt
- 2 tablespoons unsalted butter, melted
- ¼ cup all-purpose flour

Cake
- ½ cup all-purpose flour
- ¾ teaspoon baking powder
- ¼ teaspoon salt
- 2 tablespoons unsalted butter, softened
- ¼ cup granulated sugar
- 1 large egg
- ½ teaspoon vanilla extract
- 2 tablespoons sour cream
- 2 tablespoons whole milk, divided

1 Preheat air fryer to 320°F. Spray a 7" 5" baking dish with olive oil spray and set aside.

2 To make streusel: In a small bowl, mix together brown sugar, cinnamon, and salt. Pour in melted butter and mix with a fork until combined and lumpy. Slowly mix in flour, stirring with a fork until crumbly. Set aside.

3 To make cake: In a small bowl, whisk together flour, baking powder, and salt.

4 In a large bowl, combine butter and granulated sugar. Using an electric mixer on medium speed, mix until light and fluffy, about 3 minutes. Add in egg and vanilla, beating after each addition. Add sour cream and continue to mix until fully combined.

5 Add half of flour mixture and 1 tablespoon milk to the large bowl. Stir until just mixed. Add in remaining flour mixture and remaining 1 tablespoon milk and stir until just combined. Pour cake batter into prepared pan and top with streusel.

6 Air fry 15 minutes or until a toothpick inserted in the center of the cake comes out clean.

7 Remove dish from air fryer. Let cool 20 minutes before serving.

PER SERVING

CALORIES: 322 | FAT: 13g | SODIUM: 265mg | CARBOHYDRATES: 45g | FIBER: 1g | SUGAR: 27g | PROTEIN: 5g

Lemon Blueberry Coffee Cake

Made with both lemon zest and lemon juice and a generous number of blueberries that burst in your mouth, this is a fun take on a traditional coffee cake. The streusel topping gets crunchy while baking, making a nice contrast between the light flavors and crunchy topping.

Hands-On Time: 20 minutes
Cook Time: 15 minutes

Serves 4

Streusel
- 4 tablespoons packed light brown sugar
- ¼ teaspoon ground cinnamon
- ¼ teaspoon salt
- 2 tablespoons unsalted butter, melted
- ¼ cup all-purpose flour

Cake
- ½ cup all-purpose flour
- ¾ teaspoon baking powder
- ¼ teaspoon salt
- 2 tablespoons unsalted butter, softened
- ¼ cup granulated sugar
- 1 large egg
- ½ teaspoon vanilla extract
- 2 tablespoons sour cream
- 2 tablespoons whole milk, divided
- ½ cup blueberries
- 1 tablespoon lemon zest
- 1 cup confectioners' sugar
- 2 tablespoons lemon juice

1 Preheat air fryer to 320°F. Spray a 7" 5" baking dish with olive oil spray and set aside.

2 To make streusel: In a small bowl, mix together brown sugar, cinnamon, and salt. Pour in melted butter and mix with a fork until combined and lumpy. Slowly mix in flour, stirring with a fork until crumbly. Set aside.

3 To make cake: In a small bowl, whisk together flour, baking powder, and salt.

4 In a large bowl, combine butter and granulated sugar. Using an electric mixer on medium speed, mix until light and fluffy, about 3 minutes. Add in egg and vanilla, beating after each addition. Add sour cream and continue to mix until fully combined.

5 Add half of flour mixture and 1 tablespoon milk to the large bowl. Stir until just mixed. Add in remaining flour mixture and remaining 1 tablespoon milk and stir until just combined. Fold in blueberries and lemon zest. Pour cake batter into prepared pan and top with streusel.

6 Air fry 15 minutes or until a toothpick inserted in the center of the cake comes out clean.

7 Remove dish from air fryer. Let cool 20 minutes.

8 In a small bowl, whisk together confectioners' sugar and lemon juice. Drizzle over cooled coffee cake and serve.

PER SERVING

CALORIES: 432 | FAT: 13g | SODIUM: 411mg | CARBOHYDRATES: 73g | FIBER: 1g | SUGAR: 53g | PROTEIN: 5g

Orange Cranberry Muffins

These muffins are a combination of tangy cranberries and fresh orange flavor, and are light and fluffy. Fresh cranberries are difficult to procure during most times of the year, so use frozen cranberries, if needed. The berries can be folded into the batter frozen and will defrost as they bake.

Hands-On Time: 15 minutes
Cook Time: 16 minutes

Serves 6

1 cup all-purpose flour
½ cup plus 1 tablespoon granulated sugar, divided
1 large egg
2 tablespoons buttermilk
2 tablespoons no-pulp orange juice
6 tablespoons unsalted butter, melted
1 tablespoon orange zest
½ teaspoon vanilla extract
1¼ teaspoons baking powder
¼ teaspoon salt
1 cup cranberries

USING DRIED CRANBERRIES

Not able to find fresh or frozen cranberries? No problem. If you're using dried cranberries, soak them in hot water for 10 minutes. Dry them gently with a paper towel and add them to the batter as described in this recipe.

1 Preheat air fryer to 350°F. Spray a six-hole silicone egg mold with olive oil spray and set aside.

2 In a medium bowl, mix together flour, ½ cup granulated sugar, egg, buttermilk, orange juice, butter, orange zest, vanilla, baking powder, and salt. Stir until no longer dry but still lumpy.

3 Fold in cranberries. Stir just until evenly distributed.

4 Scoop mixture into prepared egg mold. Sprinkle top of batter with remaining 1 table-spoon granulated sugar. Carefully place egg mold inside air fryer.

5 Air fry 16 minutes or until a toothpick inserted in the center of a muffin comes out clean.

6 Remove egg mold from air fryer, set mold on a wire rack, and let cool 10 minutes. Serve.

PER SERVING

CALORIES: 274 | FAT: 12g | SODIUM: 212mg | CARBOHYDRATES: 38g | FIBER: 1g | SUGAR: 20g | PROTEIN: 3g

Bacon Crescent Rolls

These Bacon Crescent Rolls can be prepared ahead of time and stored in the refrigerator (they can be reheated in the air fryer at 300°F until warmed through).

Hands-On Time: 10 minutes
Cook Time: 9 minutes

Serves 4

1 (8-ounce) canister crescent roll dough
½ cup chive and onion cream cheese
4 slices cooked bacon, cut in half

1 Preheat air fryer to 325°F.

2 Roll out crescent roll dough and separate each triangle. Spread 1 tablespoon cream cheese on each triangle. Place 1 bacon piece across the center of each triangle. Roll up the triangles starting with the wide end.

3 Spray inside of air fryer with olive oil spray. Arrange prepared rolls inside air fryer, spaced 1" apart. Air fry 9 minutes, flipping halfway through, or until golden brown and cooked through.

4 Remove from air fryer and serve.

PER SERVING

CALORIES: 315 | FAT: 18g | SODIUM: 722mg | CARBOHYDRATES: 27g | FIBER: 0g | SUGAR: 8g | PROTEIN: 10g

Sausage and Cheddar Egg Muffins

Feel free to serve these muffins with a drizzle of hot sauce for a little kick.

Hands-On Time: 10 minutes
Cook Time: 17 minutes

Serves 6

6 large eggs
¾ cup whole milk
2 ounces precooked breakfast sausage links, diced
3 tablespoons shredded sharp Cheddar cheese, divided
½ teaspoon salt
¼ teaspoon ground black pepper

1 Preheat air fryer to 300°F. Spray a six-hole silicone egg mold with olive oil spray and set aside.

2 In a medium bowl, whisk eggs. Add milk, sausage, 2 tablespoons cheese, salt, and pepper and mix to combine. Pour mixture into prepared egg mold and place mold inside air fryer.

3 Air fry 16 minutes or until egg mixture is no longer jiggly, then sprinkle egg muffins with remaining 1 tablespoon cheese. Air fry an additional 1 minute or until cheese is melted.

4 Remove from air fryer and serve.

PER SERVING

CALORIES: 141 | FAT: 9g | SODIUM: 376mg | CARBOHYDRATES: 2g | FIBER: 0g | SUGAR: 2g | PROTEIN: 9g

Apple Oatmeal Muffins

The combination of fresh apples and rolled oats gives these muffins lots and lots of texture. They still come out light and airy while adding an extra bite of sweet-tart apples that are cooked to perfection. If you prefer a sweeter apple, a Gala or Honeycrisp may be substituted for the Granny Smith.

Hands-On Time: 15 minutes
Cook Time: 15 minutes

Serves 6

¾ cup all-purpose flour
¼ cup old-fashioned rolled oats
¼ cup granulated sugar
¼ cup packed light brown sugar
1 large egg
¼ cup buttermilk
6 tablespoons unsalted butter, melted
½ teaspoon vanilla extract
1¼ teaspoons baking powder
¾ teaspoon ground cinnamon
⅛ teaspoon ground nutmeg
¼ teaspoon salt
1 large Granny Smith apple, peeled, cored, and diced
1 tablespoon cinnamon sugar

MAKE YOUR OWN CINNAMON SUGAR
Create your own sweet mixture with one part cinnamon and four parts granulated sugar. Cinnamon sugar can be stored in a cool, dry place for several months. Simply store it in an old spice shaker or Mason jar.

1 Preheat air fryer to 350°F. Spray a six-hole silicone egg mold with olive oil spray and set aside.

2 In a medium bowl, mix together flour, oats, granulated sugar, brown sugar, egg, buttermilk, butter, vanilla, baking powder, cinnamon, nutmeg, and salt. Stir until no longer dry but still lumpy. Fold in apples. Stir just until evenly distributed.

3 Scoop mixture into egg mold. Sprinkle top of batter with cinnamon sugar. Carefully place egg mold inside air fryer.

4 Air fry 15 minutes or until a toothpick inserted in the center of a muffin comes out clean.

5 Remove egg mold from air fryer, set mold on a wire rack, and let cool 10 minutes. Serve.

PER SERVING

CALORIES: 282 | FAT: 12g | SODIUM: 225mg | CARBOHYDRATES: 39g | FIBER: 1g | SUGAR: 23g | PROTEIN: 4g

Applesauce Muffins

Applesauce Muffins sometimes get a bad rap as a "diet" muffin, but this recipe makes them comfort food–worthy! These muffins feature applesauce and walnuts, and they're packed with cinnamon, allspice, cloves, and nutmeg. Once baked, they are rolled in cinnamon sugar. If you can't find cinnamon sugar in the spice aisle, you can make your own (see the Apple Oatmeal Muffin recipe in this chapter).

Hands-On Time: 15 minutes
Cook Time: 15 minutes

Serves 6

1 cup all-purpose flour
½ cup granulated sugar
1 large egg
¼ cup applesauce
6 tablespoons unsalted butter, melted
½ teaspoon vanilla extract
1¼ teaspoons baking powder
½ teaspoon ground cinnamon
½ teaspoon allspice
⅛ teaspoon ground cloves
⅛ teaspoon ground nutmeg
¼ teaspoon salt
1 cup chopped walnuts
¼ cup cinnamon sugar

1 Preheat air fryer to 350°F. Spray a six-hole silicone egg mold with olive oil spray and set aside.

2 In a medium bowl, mix together flour, sugar, egg, applesauce, butter, vanilla, baking powder, cinnamon, allspice, cloves, nutmeg, and salt. Stir until no longer dry but still lumpy. Fold in walnuts. Stir just until evenly distributed.

3 Scoop mixture into prepared egg mold. Carefully place egg mold inside air fryer. Air fry 15 minutes or until a toothpick inserted in the center of a muffin comes out clean.

4 Remove egg mold from air fryer and set mold on a wire rack. Let cool 5 minutes.

5 Carefully pop muffins out of mold and roll in cinnamon sugar. Let cool an additional 5 minutes. Serve.

PER SERVING

CALORIES: 421 | **FAT:** 24g | **SODIUM:** 212mg | **CARBOHYDRATES:** 44g | **FIBER:** 2g | **SUGAR:** 25g | **PROTEIN:** 6g

Double Chocolate Muffins

These decadent muffins are great for any chocolate lover's sweet tooth! They are technically a sweet breakfast item but could pass for an afternoon snack or dessert too! For the fluffiest muffins, use room temperature eggs and milk. Simply set those items out about 30 minutes before you begin making the batter.

Hands-On Time: 15 minutes
Cook Time: 15 minutes

Serves 6

¾ cup all-purpose flour

¼ cup unsweetened cocoa powder

½ cup plus 1 tablespoon granulated sugar, divided

1 large egg

¼ cup buttermilk

6 tablespoons unsalted butter, melted

½ teaspoon vanilla extract

1¼ teaspoons baking powder

¼ teaspoon baking soda

¼ teaspoon salt

1 cup semisweet mini chocolate chips

1 Preheat air fryer to 350°F. Spray a six-hole silicone egg mold with olive oil spray and set aside.

2 In a medium bowl, mix together flour, cocoa powder, ½ cup granulated sugar, egg, buttermilk, butter, vanilla, baking powder, baking soda, and salt. Stir until no longer dry but still lumpy. Fold in chocolate chips. Stir just until evenly distributed.

3 Scoop mixture into prepared egg mold, filling ¾ full. Sprinkle top of batter with remaining 1 tablespoon granulated sugar. Carefully place egg mold inside air fryer.

4 Air fry 15 minutes or until a toothpick inserted in the center of a muffin comes out clean. Remove egg mold from air fryer, set mold on a wire rack, and let cool 10 minutes. Serve.

PER SERVING

CALORIES: 397 | **FAT:** 21g | **SODIUM:** 278mg | **CARBOHYDRATES:** 52g | **FIBER:** 3g | **SUGAR:** 35g | **PROTEIN:** 5g

Breakfast Cookies

These breakfast cookies are made with old-fashioned oats, creamy peanut butter, applesauce, mashed banana, and raisins. All of these wholesome ingredients come together to form delicious gooey and chewy cookies. This recipe is incredibly flexible: You can swap out the peanut butter for your favorite nut butter or use maple syrup for honey. The walnuts can also be swapped out for whatever nut you have on hand.

Hands-On Time: 10 minutes

Cook Time: 5 minutes (per batch)

Serves 6 (2 cookies per serving)

2 cups old-fashioned oats
½ teaspoon salt
1 teaspoon ground cinnamon
1 cup creamy peanut butter
¼ cup honey
⅓ cup unsweetened applesauce
1 large banana, peeled and mashed
½ cup raisins
½ cup dried cranberries
½ cup chopped walnuts

1 Preheat air fryer to 350°F.

2 In a large bowl, mix together all ingredients.

3 Roll ¼ cup dough at a time into a ball and then flatten slightly.

4 Spray inside of air fryer with olive oil spray before each batch. Working in batches, arrange dough pieces inside air fryer, spaced ½" apart. Air fry 5 minutes.

5 Remove cookies from air fryer and transfer to a wire rack. Let cool 10 minutes before serving.

PER SERVING

CALORIES: 572 | FAT: 31g | SODIUM: 196mg | CARBOHYDRATES: 63g | FIBER: 8g | SUGAR: 33g | PROTEIN: 16g

Scotch Eggs

A traditional Scotch egg is a hard-cooked egg that is wrapped in flavorful pork sausage, covered in crispy bread crumbs, and deep-fried. This air fryer version makes Scotch eggs perfectly crispy on the outside and tender on the inside without all of the extra oil. Although Scotch eggs are traditionally served cold in Britain, this version is best enjoyed warm. Season with salt and pepper and top with mustard, if desired.

Hands-On Time: 15 minutes
Cook Time: 12 minutes

Makes 4 eggs

- 1 pound ground pork sausage
- 1 teaspoon dried minced onion
- 1 teaspoon salt
- ¼ cup all-purpose flour
- 1 large egg, beaten
- ¾ cup panko bread crumbs
- 4 large hard-cooked eggs

HARD-COOKED EGGS IN THE AIR FRYER

Your hard-cooked eggs can be prepared in the air fryer. Simply arrange the eggs in a single layer and air fry at 270°F (or the lowest temperature available for your air fryer) for 15 minutes. Remove eggs from air fryer and place in an ice bath for 5 minutes. Finally, peel them under cool running water.

1 Preheat air fryer to 390°F.

2 In a medium bowl, combine sausage, onion, and salt. Mix well. Divide mixture into four equal parts and shape each into a ½"-thick patty.

3 In one shallow bowl, place flour. In another shallow bowl, place beaten egg. In a third shallow bowl, place bread crumbs. Roll hard-cooked eggs in flour. Place 1 hard-cooked egg in the center of each patty and wrap sausage around egg. Then dip sausage-wrapped eggs into beaten egg. Finally, dip eggs into bread crumbs until coated completely.

4 Spray inside of air fryer with olive oil spray. Arrange eggs inside air fryer so they are not touching. Air fry 12 minutes, flipping eggs halfway through. Sausage is done when it reaches an internal temperature of 145°F.

5 Remove from air fryer and serve.

PER SERVING

CALORIES: 365 | FAT: 17g | SODIUM: 753mg | CARBOHYDRATES: 22g | FIBER: 0g | SUGAR: 1g | PROTEIN: 25g

Potatoes O'Brien

This classic breakfast potato dish is excellent when cooked in the air fryer. The potatoes get extra crispy without burning. The onion and bell peppers get soft and slightly charred and are never too crunchy. The green onion garnish adds a nice fresh bite to this dish, but feel free to omit if you don't have any on hand. These potatoes can be served as a traditional breakfast dish or as a side dish at dinner. Try serving them with Filet Mignon with Garlic Herb Butter (see Chapter 6) for a hearty meal.

Hands-On Time: 15 minutes
Cook Time: 20 minutes

Serves 4

- 1½ pounds Yukon Gold potatoes, cut into ½" cubes
- 1 small green bell pepper, seeded and chopped
- 1 small red bell pepper, seeded and chopped
- 1 medium yellow onion, peeled and chopped
- 2 cloves garlic, peeled and minced
- 2 tablespoons olive oil
- 1¼ teaspoons salt
- ¼ teaspoon ground black pepper
- 2 medium green onions, thinly sliced

1 Preheat air fryer to 400°F.

2 In a large bowl, combine potatoes, bell peppers, onion, garlic, olive oil, salt, and black pepper. Mix until potatoes and peppers are evenly coated with oil and spices.

3 Place potato mixture inside air fryer. Air fry 20 minutes, shaking or turning halfway through. Potatoes are done when they are golden brown and fork-tender.

4 Remove potatoes from air fryer, top with green onions, and serve.

PER SERVING

CALORIES: 214 | FAT: 7g | SODIUM: 739mg | CARBOHYDRATES: 35g | FIBER: 5g | SUGAR: 4g | PROTEIN: 4g

Cheesy Breakfast Potatoes

Crispy russet potatoes are topped with melted Cheddar cheese and salty, crumbled bacon. These breakfast potatoes are both comforting and filling. The potatoes are simple to make by combining diced potatoes with a variety of spices and air frying until fork-tender. Then just top them with cheese and bacon and cook until cheese is melted. These potatoes pair well with eggs and taste great when topped with sliced scallions and a dollop of sour cream.

Hands-On Time: 15 minutes
Cook Time: 21 minutes

Serves 4

- 1½ pounds russet potatoes, peeled and cut into ½" cubes
- 2 tablespoons olive oil
- 1 teaspoon salt
- 1 teaspoon garlic powder
- 1 teaspoon paprika
- ½ teaspoon ground black pepper
- ½ cup shredded sharp Cheddar cheese
- 2 slices bacon, cooked and crumbled

1 Preheat air fryer to 400°F.

2 In a large bowl, combine potatoes, olive oil, salt, garlic powder, paprika, and pepper. Mix until potatoes are evenly coated with oil and spices.

3 Place potatoes inside air fryer. Air fry 20 minutes, shaking or turning halfway through.

4 Once potatoes are golden brown and fork-tender, top with cheese and bacon. Air fry an additional 1 minute or until cheese is melted.

5 Remove from air fryer and serve.

PER SERVING

CALORIES: 300 | FAT: 12g | SODIUM: 762mg | CARBOHYDRATES: 38g | FIBER: 3g | SUGAR: 3g | PROTEIN: 9g

Bacon Breakfast Casserole

This casserole serves two as a main dish but can serve more if paired with something extra like Orange Cranberry Muffins (see recipe in this chapter).

Hands-On Time: 15 minutes
Cook Time: 20 minutes

Serves 2

1½ cups frozen shredded
    hash browns
2 slices bacon, chopped
4 large eggs
2 tablespoons whole milk
¼ cup shredded sharp
    Cheddar cheese
½ teaspoon salt
⅛ teaspoon ground black
    pepper

1 Preheat air fryer to 400°F. Spray a 7" cake pan with olive oil spray.

2 Arrange hash browns in cake pan and top with bacon. Place pan inside air fryer and fry 10 minutes.

3 In a medium bowl, combine eggs, milk, cheese, salt, and pepper. Whisk until fully combined. Pour egg mixture over potatoes, lower temperature to 320°F, and air fry an additional 10 minutes or until eggs are set.

4 Remove cake pan from air fryer. Let rest 10 minutes. Serve.

PER SERVING

CALORIES: 381 | FAT: 17g | SODIUM: 1,016mg | CARBOHYDRATES: 30g | FIBER: 2g | SUGAR: 1g | PROTEIN: 23g

Sausage Pancake Muffins

These muffins can be frozen for up to 3 months. Let them defrost at room temperature for about 30 minutes and reheat in the air fryer for 2 to 3 minutes at 300°F.

Hands-On Time: 10 minutes
Cook Time: 7 minutes (per batch)

Makes 12 muffins

1 cup pancake mix
¾ cup water
1 teaspoon vanilla extract
12 fully cooked turkey
    sausage links, sliced ¼"
    thick

1 Preheat air fryer to 320°F. Spray a six-hole silicone egg mold with olive oil spray and set aside.

2 In a bowl, combine pancake mix, water, and vanilla. Mix well and add sausage.

3 Working in batches, scoop pancake mix into prepared egg mold, filling ⅔ of the way full.

4 Air fry 7 minutes or until a toothpick inserted in the center comes out clean.

5 Remove egg mold from air fryer and place on a wire rack. Let cool 10 minutes. Serve.

PER SERVING

CALORIES: 144 | FAT: 5g | SODIUM: 459mg | CARBOHYDRATES: 7g | FIBER: 0g | SUGAR: 2g | PROTEIN: 14g

Biscuits and Gravy Casserole

You may have had good biscuits and gravy, but this casserole takes it up a notch! If you like your dishes on the milder side, swap the hot Italian sausage for mild Italian sausage and the peppered gravy for traditional country gravy. This casserole also makes great leftovers. Reheat in the air fryer at 300° until heated through, about 5 minutes.

Hands-On Time: 20 minutes
Cook Time: 30 minutes

Serves 2

- ½ (16-ounce) canister refrigerated biscuit dough
- ½ pound ground hot Italian sausage, browned
- ¼ cup shredded sharp Cheddar cheese
- 3 large eggs
- ¼ cup whole milk
- ¾ teaspoon salt
- ¼ teaspoon ground black pepper
- 1 cup prepared peppered country gravy, from 1 (2.75-ounce) packet country gravy mix

1 Preheat air fryer to 320°F. Spray a 7" cake pan with olive oil spray.

2 Cut four biscuit dough pieces into quarters. Arrange biscuit dough in an even layer inside cake pan. Sprinkle sausage and cheese over biscuit dough.

3 In a medium bowl, whisk together eggs, milk, salt, and pepper. Pour egg mixture over sausage and cheese. Then drizzle gravy on top.

4 Place pan in air fryer and air fry 30 minutes or until casserole reaches an internal temperature of 160°F.

5 Remove pan from air fryer. Let set 10 minutes. Serve.

PER SERVING

CALORIES: 905 | FAT: 46g | SODIUM: 3,608mg | CARBOHYDRATES: 75g | FIBER: 3g | SUGAR: 12g | PROTEIN: 36g

3

Appetizers and Snacks

Appetizers and snacks in the air fryer are just as delicious as their deep-fried counterparts. This chapter includes many classic comfort food recipes that are traditionally soaked in oil. Each snack comes out crispy and tender in a fraction of the time! There are delicious savory snacks like Air Fryer Dill Pickle Spears, Egg Rolls, and Loaded Sweet Potato Skins. If you are looking for something sweeter, the Cinnamon Almonds or Chocolate Chip Granola Bars will be right up your alley! Heading to a potluck? Bring along some Sticky Barbecue Wings, Bourbon Meatballs, or Deviled Eggs. All of the recipes are delicious and will satisfy that comfort food craving.

Air Fryer Dill Pickle Spears

Fried pickles are a zesty, crunchy treat! This recipe uses dill pickle spears and double breads them with a spiced bread crumb mixture that enhances the flavor of the pickles. These air fryer pickles are best eaten the same day they're made and can be served with ranch dressing as a dipping sauce. Remember: It's very important to dry the pickles fully, as that will help the batter cling to the pickles.

Hands-On Time: 20 minutes
Cook Time: 9 minutes (per batch)

Serves 6 (2 spears each)

1 (24-ounce) jar dill pickle
    spears
½ cup all-purpose flour
2 teaspoons salt, divided
1 teaspoon ground black
    pepper, divided
4 large eggs, beaten
2 cups panko bread crumbs
1 teaspoon paprika
1 teaspoon garlic powder
1 teaspoon onion powder

FRYING PICKLE SLICES

If you prefer air fryer pickle slices, you can substitute the dill pickle spears with dill pickle slices. Follow the recipe as directed, making sure to space out the slices in the air fryer. More batches may be required.

1   Preheat air fryer to 400°F.

2   Remove pickles from jar and dry with paper towels.

3   In one shallow bowl, place flour and mix in ½ teaspoon salt and ¼ teaspoon pepper. In another shallow bowl, place eggs. In a third shallow bowl, place bread crumbs and mix in remaining 1½ teaspoons salt, remaining ¾ teaspoon pepper, paprika, garlic powder, and onion powder.

4   Dredge each pickle spear in flour mixture, turning to coat. Then dip pickle in eggs, lightly shaking to remove any excess. Finally, dip pickle in bread crumb mixture, turning to evenly coat, then dip coated pickle again in eggs and then bread crumbs.

5   Spray inside of air fryer with olive oil spray before each batch. Working in batches, arrange pickles inside air fryer so they are not touching. Air fry 9 minutes.

6   Remove from air fryer, then serve.

PER SERVING

CALORIES: 120 | FAT: 2g | SODIUM: 1,014mg | CARBOHYDRATES: 20g | FIBER: 1g | SUGAR: 2g | PROTEIN: 5g

Sticky Barbecue Wings

You can't beat barbecue wings cooked in the air fryer! The wings are cooked until they are fall-off-the-bone tender and coated with a sweet and tangy sauce. You can make them ahead of time and reheat them in the air fryer or enjoy them right away. They taste great on their own or served with blue cheese dressing for dipping. Sticky Barbecue Wings are a great appetizer but can also be served as a main dish. You decide!

Hands-On Time: 20 minutes
Cook Time: 35 minutes

Serves 5

1 teaspoon salt
½ teaspoon garlic powder
½ teaspoon paprika
¼ teaspoon ground black pepper
10 chicken wing sections (2 pounds total)
1 cup barbecue sauce
¼ cup packed light brown sugar
¼ cup honey
2 tablespoons ketchup
1 teaspoon Worcestershire sauce
1 teaspoon low-sodium soy sauce

1 Preheat air fryer to 380°F.

2 In a small bowl, mix salt, garlic powder, paprika, and pepper. Sprinkle seasoning over chicken wings.

3 Spray inside of air fryer with olive oil spray. Arrange chicken wings inside air fryer so they're not touching. Air fry 20 minutes.

4 In a small saucepan over medium heat, combine barbecue sauce, brown sugar, honey, ketchup, Worcestershire sauce, and soy sauce. Bring sauce to a simmer, stirring constantly. Continue stirring and cook 5 minutes. Reduce heat to low, stirring occasionally, until ready to use.

5 Once chicken has finished cooking, remove from air fryer and brush sauce onto one side of wings. Air fry 5 minutes, then flip wings over and brush the other side with remaining sauce. Air fry an additional 5 minutes. Wings are ready when the internal temperature reaches 165°F.

6 Remove from air fryer, then serve.

PER SERVING

CALORIES: 633 | FAT: 28g | SODIUM: 1,323mg | CARBOHYDRATES: 51g | FIBER: 1g | SUGAR: 35g | PROTEIN: 41g

Garlic Toast

This Garlic Toast takes just 5 minutes to cook in the air fryer! Make sure to purchase the thick-sliced Texas toast loaf in the bread aisle, not the premade frozen toast with the same name.

Hands-On Time: 10 minutes
Cook Time: 5 minutes (per batch)

Serves 4

4 tablespoons unsalted butter, softened
2 tablespoons minced garlic
1 teaspoon salt
1 teaspoon garlic powder
1 tablespoon minced fresh flat-leaf Italian parsley
8 (1"-thick) slices Texas toast

1 Preheat air fryer to 400°F.

2 In a small bowl, mix together butter, minced garlic, salt, garlic powder, and parsley.

3 Spread butter mixture on one side of each bread slice.

4 Arrange bread slices inside air fryer, spaced ½" apart (you may need to work in batches). Air fry 5 minutes.

5 Remove from air fryer and serve.

PER SERVING

CALORIES: 296 | FAT: 13g | SODIUM: 927mg | CARBOHYDRATES: 37g | FIBER: 2g | SUGAR: 4g | PROTEIN: 7g

Grilled Cheese

It's important to use a toothpick to hold the sandwich together; otherwise, you risk your bread flying around the air fryer before it has a chance to cook.

Hands-On Time: 10 minutes
Cook Time: 8 minutes (per batch)

Serves 4

4 tablespoons salted butter, room temperature
8 (¾"-thick) slices white bread
8 (1-ounce) slices American cheese
1 large Roma tomato, sliced into 8 (½") slices

1 Preheat air fryer to 400°F.

2 Spread butter on one side of each bread slice.

3 Build four sandwiches by placing 2 slices cheese and 2 slices tomato on 4 unbuttered bread slices. Top with remaining bread slices, buttered sides facing out. Hold each sandwich together with a toothpick.

4 Arrange sandwiches inside air fryer so they're not touching (you may need to work in batches).

5 Air fry 8 minutes, flipping halfway through.

6 Remove from air fryer and serve.

PER SERVING

CALORIES: 402 | FAT: 20g | SODIUM: 1,149mg | CARBOHYDRATES: 37g | FIBER: 2g | SUGAR: 9g | PROTEIN: 15g

Mini Corn Dogs

With this recipe, you can enjoy your favorite carnival food at home! These Mini Corn Dogs are cooked in a delicious cornmeal batter, which adds the perfect amount of sweetness that pairs nicely with the salty hot dogs. Note: These Mini Corn Dogs will not be perfectly rounded on each side. The side where they sit on the air fryer will be flat. Although they come out looking homemade, they still taste amazing. Serve them with your favorite condiments.

Hands-On Time: 30 minutes
Cook Time: 9 minutes

Serves 4

1 cup cornmeal
1¼ cups all-purpose flour, divided
1 cup granulated sugar
4 teaspoons baking powder
½ teaspoon salt
⅛ teaspoon ground black pepper
1 large egg
1 cup buttermilk
4 (3.5-ounce) beef hot dogs, cut into thirds

1 In a medium bowl, combine cornmeal, 1 cup flour, sugar, baking powder, salt, and pepper. Mix well.

2 Add in egg and buttermilk. Mix until batter is smooth. Refrigerate 20 minutes.

3 Preheat air fryer to 370°F.

4 Dip each hot dog piece into remaining ¼ cup flour and then into the prepared batter. Make sure hot dog pieces are completely coated with batter.

5 Arrange mini corn dogs inside air fryer so they are not touching. Air fry 9 minutes or until brown and crispy with an internal temperature of 160°F.

6 Remove from air fryer. Serve.

PER SERVING

CALORIES: 698 | FAT: 27g | SODIUM: 1,637mg | CARBOHYDRATES: 86g | FIBER: 3g | SUGAR: 41g | PROTEIN: 19g

Bacon Avocado Fries

When choosing bacon, avoid a thick cut, which will take longer to cook. Choose avocados with a greenish-black skin. The fruit should be firm to the touch but not rock-hard. Do not use squishy (or fully ripened) avocados for these fries.

Hands-On Time: 10 minutes
Cook Time: 8 minutes

Serves 4

2 large avocados, peeled, pitted, and each sliced into 8 equal slices
16 slices bacon

1 Preheat air fryer to 400°F.

2 Wrap each avocado slice with 1 slice bacon and secure with a toothpick.

3 Spray inside of air fryer with olive oil spray. Arrange avocado fries inside air fryer so they are not touching. Air fry 8 minutes or until bacon is cooked through.

4 Remove avocado fries from air fryer, remove toothpicks, and serve.

PER SERVING

CALORIES: 286 | FAT: 21g | SODIUM: 654mg | CARBOHYDRATES: 6g | FIBER: 5g | SUGAR: 0g | PROTEIN: 16g

Savory Mixed Nuts

These Savory Mixed Nuts taste great on their own, added to a cheese board, or on top of a salad.

Hands-On Time: 10 minutes
Cook Time: 5 minutes

Serves 8

2 cups unsalted mixed nuts
⅛ cup olive oil
1 teaspoon salt
1 teaspoon dried rosemary
1 teaspoon dried oregano
½ teaspoon cayenne pepper
¼ teaspoon ground black pepper

1 Preheat air fryer to 320°F.

2 In a medium bowl, combine all ingredients. Mix well.

3 Spray inside of air fryer with olive oil spray. Arrange nuts inside air fryer in an even layer. Air fry 5 minutes or until crisp.

4 Remove from air fryer. Serve warm or allow nuts to cool completely, about 30 minutes, and store in an airtight container at room temperature up to 1 week.

PER SERVING

CALORIES: 234 | FAT: 20g | SODIUM: 294mg | CARBOHYDRATES: 9g | FIBER: 3g | SUGAR: 0g | PROTEIN: 6g

Loaded Sweet Potato Skins

This is a tasty spin on a classic appetizer that you won't want to miss! The sweet potatoes are made perfectly crisp in the air fryer. Then the filling is mixed with buttermilk and seasonings to enhance the flavor of the sweet potato, without making it extra sweet. Finally, it's loaded with delicious toppings: two types of cheese, crumbled bacon, sour cream, and chives. The result is a mouthwatering appetizer that you will want to make again and again.

Hands-On Time: 20 minutes
Cook Time: 30 minutes

Serves 4

- 4 medium sweet potatoes
- 1 tablespoon olive oil
- ¼ cup buttermilk
- ½ teaspoon salt
- ¼ teaspoon ground black pepper
- ½ cup shredded mozzarella cheese
- ½ cup shredded sharp Cheddar cheese
- 4 strips bacon, cooked and crumbled
- ¼ cup sour cream
- 2 tablespoons chopped chives

1 Preheat air fryer to 400°F.

2 Poke sweet potatoes all over with the tines of a fork and place inside air fryer. Air fry 20 minutes or until fork-tender.

3 Remove sweet potatoes from air fryer and slice in half. Scoop flesh out from potatoes, leaving some sweet potato flesh around the edges of each potato skin. Add flesh to a medium bowl.

4 Brush potato skins with olive oil and place inside air fryer, skin side down. Air fry 5 minutes.

5 Add buttermilk, salt, and pepper to bowl with sweet potato flesh. Mash potato and mix well.

6 Fill each sweet potato skin with a scoop of mashed sweet potato mixture. Top with mozzarella and Cheddar cheeses. Air fry an additional 5 minutes.

7 Remove from air fryer and top each sweet potato skin with each remaining ingredient: crumbled bacon, sour cream, and chives. Serve warm.

PER SERVING

CALORIES: 311 | FAT: 15g | SODIUM: 711mg | CARBOHYDRATES: 29g | FIBER: 4g | SUGAR: 7g | PROTEIN: 12g

Porcupine Meatballs

These tender treats resemble little porcupines, explaining their adorable name. They are served in a delicious tomato soup–based sauce that complements the meatballs perfectly. They can be enjoyed on their own (served on toothpicks) or over a bed of creamy mashed potatoes. The meatballs can be prepped and shaped, covered in plastic wrap, and stored in the refrigerator for up to 2 days before cooking.

Hands-On Time: 15 minutes
Cook Time: 9 minutes

Serves 4

1 pound (93% lean) ground beef
½ cup cooked white rice
¼ cup diced yellow onion
1 large egg, beaten
1 tablespoon chopped fresh flat-leaf Italian parsley
1 teaspoon salt
½ teaspoon garlic powder
¼ teaspoon paprika
¼ teaspoon ground black pepper
1 (10.75-ounce) can condensed tomato soup
¼ cup water
1 tablespoon Worcestershire sauce

1 Preheat air fryer to 360°F.

2 In a large bowl, combine ground beef, rice, onion, egg, parsley, salt, garlic powder, paprika, and pepper. Mix well and shape into twenty meatballs.

3 Spray inside of air fryer with olive oil spray. Place meatballs inside air fryer and air fry 6 minutes, turning halfway through.

4 Pour tomato soup, water, and Worcester-shire sauce in a medium bowl and stir until combined.

5 Place meatballs in a 7" cake pan. Pour sauce over meatballs.

6 Place pan inside air fryer and air fry 3 minutes or until sauce is hot and bubbly. Meatballs are done when they reach an internal temperature of 160°F.

7 Remove pan from air fryer. Serve.

FREEZING TIP

These meatballs can be prepared ahead of time and stored in the freezer. Simply prepare the meatballs but do not air fry. Place in a freezer-safe bag or container and freeze for up to 3 months. Prepare the sauce when you are ready to cook the frozen meatballs, adding 5–10 minutes to the final cook time.

PER SERVING

CALORIES: 282 | **FAT:** 9g | **SODIUM:** 1,003mg | **CARBOHYDRATES:** 21g | **FIBER:** 1g | **SUGAR:** 7g | **PROTEIN:** 29g

Cinnamon Almonds

Cinnamon almonds, also known as candied almonds, are crunchy roasted almonds covered in a sweet coating. They are a fantastic treat at parties and also make sweet homemade gifts. They taste great warm and fresh from the oven, or once cooled, served as an on-the-go snack or even as a salad topper. Once they're completely cooled, they can be stored in an airtight container at room temperature for up to 1 week or frozen for up to 3 months.

Hands-On Time: 20 minutes
Cook Time: 25 minutes

Serves 8

1 large egg white
1 teaspoon cold water
1 teaspoon vanilla extract
2 cups raw unsalted almonds
½ cup packed light brown sugar
1½ teaspoons ground cinnamon
¼ teaspoon salt

1 Preheat air fryer to 300°F.

2 In a large bowl, combine egg white and water. Beat, using an electric mixer on medium speed, until very frothy but not stiff, about 3 minutes. Pour in vanilla and beat again until combined.

3 Add almonds to egg white mixture and stir gently until evenly coated.

4 In a medium bowl, mix brown sugar, cinnamon, and salt.

5 Pour sugar mixture over almonds and stir until almonds are covered with sugar and seasoning.

6 Spray inside of air fryer with olive oil spray.

7 Arrange almonds inside air fryer in an even layer. Air fry 25 minutes or until crisp, stirring halfway through.

8 Remove from air fryer. Serve warm or allow almonds to cool completely, about 30 minutes, and store in an airtight container at room temperature up to 1 week.

PER SERVING

CALORIES: 263 | FAT: 17g | SODIUM: 83mg | CARBOHYDRATES: 22g | FIBER: 5g | SUGAR: 15g | PROTEIN: 8g

Bourbon Meatballs

Bourbon Meatballs are a tasty cocktail meatball made with a delicious combination of beef and pork and filled with bacon and chopped onion. The bourbon sauce is a mixture of bourbon, apricot preserves, sweet chili sauce, molasses, brown sugar, and barbecue sauce. The sweet and tangy sauce is the perfect pairing with the moist and tender meatballs. If you need to reheat the meatballs, place them in a cake pan with the sauce and cover in foil. Air fry at 300° until warm in the center, about 5 minutes.

Hands-On Time: 20 minutes
Cook Time: 16 minutes

Serves 6

½ pound (93% lean) ground beef
½ pound (93% lean) ground pork
2 slices bacon, chopped
1 large egg
½ cup panko bread crumbs
½ cup chopped yellow onion
1 teaspoon salt
¼ teaspoon ground black pepper
1 cup apricot preserves
¼ cup packed light brown sugar
2 tablespoons sweet chili sauce
½ cup bourbon
½ cup barbecue sauce
1 tablespoon molasses
¼ cup water

1 Preheat air fryer to 360°F.

2 In a large bowl, combine beef, pork, bacon, egg, bread crumbs, onion, salt, and pepper. Mix well until fully combined. Roll meat into twenty (1") meatballs.

3 Place meatballs inside air fryer in a single layer. Air fry 6 minutes, flipping halfway through. Meatballs are done when they reach an internal temperature of 160°F.

4 In a medium saucepan over medium-high heat, add apricot preserves, brown sugar, chili sauce, bourbon, barbecue sauce, molasses, and water. Bring to a simmer and let cook 10 minutes, stirring often. Remove from heat.

5 Remove meatballs from air fryer. Add to sauce and gently stir to coat. Serve immediately.

PER SERVING

CALORIES: 434 | FAT: 6g | SODIUM: 873mg | CARBOHYDRATES: 70g | FIBER: 2g | SUGAR: 47g | PROTEIN: 22g

Egg Rolls

These Egg Rolls taste just as good as the ones your family ordered from your local Chinese restaurant when you were growing up. The egg roll wrappers get extra crispy, and they're filled with a delicious combination of pork, ginger, garlic, and cabbage. Premade coleslaw mix can be used in place of the shredded cabbage and carrots. The ground pork can also be substituted with ground beef or turkey.

Hands-On Time: 15 minutes
Cook Time: 15 minutes

Makes 8

1 pound (93% lean) ground pork
2 cups shredded cabbage
¼ cup shredded carrots
2 green onions, sliced
1 tablespoon minced garlic
2 teaspoons ground ginger
1 teaspoon low-sodium soy sauce
2 tablespoons all-purpose flour
2 tablespoons water
8 (7") egg roll wrappers

FREEZING EGG ROLLS

Freeze uncooked egg rolls by preparing and filling the egg rolls and arranging them in a single layer on a baking sheet. Freeze 1 hour and then transfer to a freezer-safe container or bag. To cook, air fry frozen egg rolls 10–12 minutes.

1   Place pork, cabbage, carrots, green onions, garlic, ginger, and soy sauce in a medium skillet over medium-high heat. Cook, stirring constantly, until pork is browned and the cabbage is wilted, about 7 minutes.

2   In a small bowl, whisk together flour and water until a paste forms.

3   Preheat air fryer to 360°F.

4   Lay out egg roll wrappers so one corner is pointing toward you like a diamond. Fill the center of each wrapper with ¼ cup filling. Fold the bottom corner over the filling, followed by the two side corners. Brush a small amount of flour paste on the top corner. Roll egg roll wrapper up and away from you and onto the top corner to seal.

5   Spray inside of air fryer with olive oil spray. Arrange egg rolls inside air fryer (seam side down) so they are not touching. Air fry 8 minutes, flipping halfway through. Egg rolls are done when they reach an internal temperature of 145°F.

6   Remove from air fryer. Serve.

PER SERVING

CALORIES: 182 | FAT: 2g | SODIUM: 239mg | CARBOHYDRATES: 22g | FIBER: 1g | SUGAR: 1g | PROTEIN: 22g

Bruschetta

Bruschetta is a well-loved appetizer, and for good reason. The crusty, crunchy bread slices topped with tomato, fresh basil, and Parmesan can't be beat. The air fryer makes the French bread extra crispy and cooks it quickly. Make sure to remove the seeds from the Roma tomatoes, otherwise the bread will get soggy. Freshly grated Parmesan cheese is worth the extra work, as the flavor will be much stronger than the pre-shredded Parmesan cheese sold at the grocery store.

Hands-On Time: 20 minutes
Cook Time: 3 minutes (per batch)

Serves 8

- 1 loaf French bread
- 2 tablespoons olive oil
- 8 Roma tomatoes
- ⅓ cup chopped fresh basil
- 2 cloves garlic, peeled and minced
- 2 tablespoons balsamic vinegar
- ½ teaspoon salt
- ¼ teaspoon ground black pepper
- ½ cup grated Parmesan cheese

1. Preheat air fryer to 375°F.

2. Brush each side of French bread loaf with 1 tablespoon olive oil. Slice bread into 8 even slices. Arrange bread in a single layer inside air fryer (you may need to work in batches). Air fry 3 minutes or until golden.

3. Slice Roma tomatoes in half and scoop out seeds. Dice tomatoes and place in a medium bowl. Add basil, garlic, balsamic vinegar, salt, and pepper. Stir to combine.

4. Remove bread from air fryer. Top each piece of toasted bread with tomato mixture and sprinkle with Parmesan cheese. Serve.

PER SERVING

CALORIES: 156 | FAT: 5g | SODIUM: 450mg | CARBOHYDRATES: 21g | FIBER: 1g | SUGAR: 4g | PROTEIN: 6g

Candied Pecans

Candied Pecans are the perfect sweet and crunchy snack. This is a simple recipe that cooks much faster than in the oven, and the Candied Pecans can be stored for a week!

Hands-On Time: 10 minutes
Cook Time: 8 minutes

Serves 8

2 cups unsalted pecan halves
¼ cup packed light brown sugar
2 tablespoons pure maple syrup
1 teaspoon ground cinnamon
1 teaspoon ground ginger
½ teaspoon salt
⅛ teaspoon ground nutmeg

1 Preheat air fryer to 330°F.

2 In a medium bowl, combine all ingredients and mix well.

3 Spray inside of air fryer with olive oil spray. Arrange pecans inside air fryer in an even layer. Air fry 8 minutes or until crisp, stirring halfway through.

4 Remove from air fryer. Serve warm or allow nuts to cool completely, about 30 minutes, and store in an airtight container at room temperature up to 1 week.

PER SERVING

CALORIES: 211 | **FAT:** 17g | **SODIUM:** 147mg | **CARBOHYDRATES:** 14g | **FIBER:** 3g | **SUGAR:** 11g | **PROTEIN:** 2g

Garlic-Roasted Cherry Tomatoes

These roasted cherry tomatoes can be served on their own or as toppings to salads or pasta.

Hands-On Time: 10 minutes
Cook Time: 5 minutes

Serves 4

2 cups cherry tomatoes
1 tablespoon olive oil
1 teaspoon salt
½ teaspoon crushed red pepper
½ teaspoon ground black pepper
1 tablespoon minced garlic
1 tablespoon salted butter
1 tablespoon minced fresh basil

1 Preheat air fryer to 350°F.

2 Place cherry tomatoes in a 7" cake pan. Top with olive oil, salt, crushed red pepper, and black pepper. Stir to coat tomatoes.

3 Place cake pan inside air fryer and air fry 4 minutes, stirring halfway through.

4 Add garlic and butter to tomatoes and air fry an additional 1 minute or until butter is melted.

5 Remove pan from air fryer, stir tomatoes, and sprinkle with basil. Serve.

PER SERVING

CALORIES: 71 | **FAT:** 6g | **SODIUM:** 607mg | **CARBOHYDRATES:** 4g | **FIBER:** 1g | **SUGAR:** 2g | **PROTEIN:** 1g

Crispy Chickpeas

Air fryer chickpeas are a crunchy, delicious, and filling snack. They taste great on their own or on top of a salad for an extra boost of protein. It's important to dry the chickpeas as much as possible before adding the seasoning. Keep an eye on the chickpeas for the last few minutes of cooking to make sure they don't burn. The chickpeas are ready as soon as they start turning golden brown.

Hands-On Time: 10 minutes
Cook Time: 14 minutes

Serves 4

1 (15-ounce) can chickpeas
1 teaspoon olive oil
1 teaspoon garlic salt
1 teaspoon cayenne pepper
¼ teaspoon salt

1   Preheat air fryer to 380°F.

2   Drain chickpeas and pour onto two layers of paper towels. Dry chickpeas as much as possible.

3   In a medium bowl, combine all ingredients and toss to evenly coat.

4   Arrange chickpeas inside air fryer in an even layer. Air fry 14 minutes or until golden brown, shaking or turning halfway through.

5   Remove from air fryer. Serve.

PER SERVING

CALORIES: 102 | FAT: 2g | SODIUM: 776mg | CARBOHYDRATES: 15g | FIBER: 4g | SUGAR: 3g | PROTEIN: 5g

Chocolate Chip Granola Bars

Once prepared and cooled, these granola bars can be individually wrapped in parchment paper and tied with twine to make them a portable snack. They can be stored in an air-tight container at room temperature for up to 1 week. When looking for rolled oats, make sure to buy the old-fashioned variety and not quick-cooking oats, as they will not cook at the same rate.

Hands-On Time: 20 minutes
Cook Time: 12 minutes

Serves 12

- 1½ cups old-fashioned rolled oats
- ½ cup oat flour
- ¼ cup packed light brown sugar
- ¼ teaspoon salt
- ⅓ cup honey
- ¼ cup unsalted butter
- 1 teaspoon vanilla extract
- 1 cup semisweet mini chocolate chips

1 Preheat air fryer to 320°F. Line a 7" cake pan with parchment paper, allowing the paper to cover sides of pan by about 2".

2 In a large bowl, combine oats, oat flour, brown sugar, and salt. Mix until combined.

3 In a medium saucepan over medium heat, heat honey and butter until butter is melted and begins to bubble. Let cook, stirring constantly, 2 minutes. Mix in vanilla and remove from heat.

4 Pour honey mixture into oat mixture and mix well. Fold in chocolate chips.

5 Pour mixture into prepared cake pan. Top with another piece of parchment paper and press down until granola mixture is smooth and even. Place cake pan inside air fryer and air fry 10 minutes or until golden around the edges.

6 Remove cake pan from air fryer and let cool on a wire rack 30 minutes. Refrigerate 30 minutes.

7 Remove granola from pan by gently pulling up on the edges of the parchment paper. Place granola on a cutting board and peel away parchment paper. Cut into twelve equal pieces, then serve. Store in an airtight container at room temperature up to 1 week.

PER SERVING

CALORIES: 205 | FAT: 9g | SODIUM: 52mg | CARBOHYDRATES: 31g | FIBER: 2g | SUGAR: 20g | PROTEIN: 3g

Barbecue Potato Chips

The air fryer really excels at cooking homemade potato chips. This recipe takes the classic potato chip and adds a tantalizing barbecue spice mixture that turns plain chips into a mouthwatering snack you won't want to put down. Making homemade potato chips does take a bit of time, but most of it is hands-off, and it's well worth it when you bite into one of these crunchy chips.

Hands-On Time: 30 minutes
Cook Time: 7 minutes

Serves 4

2 large russet potatoes,
    sliced into ⅛"-thick slices
1 tablespoon paprika
2 teaspoons packed light
    brown sugar
1½ teaspoons salt
1 teaspoon celery salt
1 teaspoon garlic powder
½ teaspoon ground black
    pepper
6 tablespoons olive oil

CAN I MAKE PLAIN POTATO CHIPS?

If you are craving the classic potato chip flavor, simply stick to three ingredients: potatoes, salt, and olive oil.

1 Place sliced potatoes in a large bowl and cover with cold water. Let sit 20 minutes.

2 Drain potatoes and dry well with paper towels.

3 Preheat air fryer to 360°F.

4 In a small bowl, mix together paprika, brown sugar, salt, celery salt, garlic powder, and pepper.

5 Place dried potatoes in a large bowl and top with olive oil and spice mixture. Stir until evenly coated. Place potatoes inside air fryer and air fry 7 minutes, shaking or turning halfway through.

6 Remove from air fryer. Serve.

PER SERVING

CALORIES: 334 | FAT: 20g | SODIUM: 1,178mg | CARBOHYDRATES: 36g | FIBER: 4g | SUGAR: 4g | PROTEIN: 4g

Queso Dip

This classic cheese and chorizo dip is easy to make in the air fryer. It's cheesy, meaty, and just a bit spicy! Serve it with crispy tortilla chips or raw vegetables like carrots and celery. Queso Dip also makes an appetizing filling for tacos, burritos, or quesadillas. Leftover dip can be stored in the refrigerator for up to 3 days. It can be reheated in the air fryer at 300°F for 5 minutes or until warmed in the center. Top with cilantro if you'd like.

Hands-On Time: 10 minutes
Cook Time: 10 minutes

Serves 4

2 cups shredded American cheese
1 cup shredded pepper jack cheese
1 pound ground chorizo
¼ cup whole milk
1 medium jalapeño, seeded and minced
1 (15.5-ounce) can diced tomatoes with chilies
2 teaspoons garlic powder
1 teaspoon onion powder

1 Preheat air fryer to 350°F. Spray inside of cake pan with olive oil spray.

2 Arrange cheeses on the bottom of a 7" cake pan. Top with chorizo, milk, jalapeño, tomatoes, garlic powder, and onion powder.

3 Place pan inside air fryer and air fry 10 minutes, stirring halfway through.

4 Remove pan from air fryer. Serve.

PER SERVING

CALORIES: 772 | FAT: 52g | SODIUM: 2,997mg | CARBOHYDRATES: 22g | FIBER: 1g | SUGAR: 12g | PROTEIN: 46g

Onion Blossom

The trick to making this Onion Blossom is double-dipping the onion in the batter and allowing it to set in the freezer before air frying. Vidalia onions are the best for this recipe, but any large sweet onion will work.

Hands-On Time: 35 minutes
Cook Time: 20 minutes

Serves 4

Onion Blossom
1 large Vidalia onion
½ cup all-purpose flour
2 large eggs
1 cup buttermilk
1 cup panko bread crumbs
2 teaspoons paprika
1 teaspoon salt
1 teaspoon garlic powder
1 teaspoon onion powder

Dipping Sauce
½ cup mayonnaise
2 tablespoons horseradish
2 teaspoons ketchup
¼ teaspoon paprika
¼ teaspoon salt
⅛ teaspoon ground black pepper
⅛ teaspoon cayenne pepper

1 To make blossom: Cut ¾" off bottom of onion and peel off skin. Place onion on the cut side.

2 Slice 3/4 of the way down the center of the onion, leaving the base intact. Make six cuts on each half of the onion, cutting about halfway down, so there are twelve total sections. Gently spread the onion out so it looks like a blooming flower.

3 In a small shallow bowl, place flour. In another small shallow bowl, add eggs and buttermilk and whisk to combine. In a third small shallow bowl, place bread crumbs and mix in paprika, salt, garlic powder, and onion powder.

4 Dredge onion in flour, turning to coat. Then dip onion in egg mixture, gently shaking to remove any excess. Finally, dip onion in bread crumb mixture, turning to evenly coat.

5 Place prepared onion in freezer on a freezer-safe plate 20 minutes.

6 Preheat air fryer to 370°F.

7 Spray inside of air fryer with olive oil spray. Place onion inside air fryer and air fry 20 minutes or until tender all the way through.

8 To make sauce: In a small bowl, combine mayonnaise, horseradish, ketchup, paprika, salt, black pepper, and cayenne pepper.

9 Remove onion from air fryer. Serve with dipping sauce.

PER SERVING

CALORIES: 365 | FAT: 23g | SODIUM: 771mg | CARBOHYDRATES: 32g | FIBER: 3g | SUGAR: 8g | PROTEIN: 7g

Deviled Eggs

Make this crowd-pleasing appetizer in a few simple steps. Simply air fry the eggs to hard-cook them and then whip up the tasty filling. These Deviled Eggs are made with a simple and delicious combination of mayonnaise, mustard, and white vinegar. They're seasoned to perfection and finished with a sprinkling of paprika. If you want to make the Deviled Eggs extra special, top them with some bacon bits before serving.

Hands-On Time: 15 minutes
Cook Time: 15 minutes

Serves 6

6 large eggs
4 cups water
2 cups ice
⅛ cup mayonnaise
⅛ cup yellow mustard
1 teaspoon white vinegar
⅛ teaspoon salt
⅛ teaspoon ground black pepper
¼ teaspoon paprika

WHY "DEVILED"?

The term "deviled" originated in the 1800s and was originally used to refer to boiled or fried foods that were heavily seasoned or fried. It originated in Great Britain, but eventually made it to America, and is primarily used when referring to deviled eggs.

1 Preheat air fryer to 270°F.

2 Arrange eggs in a single layer inside air fryer. Air fry 15 minutes.

3 Remove cooked eggs from air fryer and place in a large bowl, then add water and ice. Let sit 10 minutes.

4 Remove eggs from ice bath and peel under cold running water.

5 Slice eggs in half and carefully scoop out yolk. Place all yolks in a medium bowl. Add mayonnaise, mustard, vinegar, salt, and pepper. Mix well.

6 Place 1 tablespoon yolk mixture in the center of each sliced egg. Sprinkle egg halves with paprika and serve.

PER SERVING

CALORIES: 112 | **FAT:** 8g | **SODIUM:** 196mg | **CARBOHYDRATES:** 1g | **FIBER:** 0g | **SUGAR:** 1g | **PROTEIN:** 7g

Bunless Burger Bites

Serve these burger bites—mini hamburgers served on a toothpick with lettuce, cherry tomatoes, and dill pickle slices—as a fun handheld appetizer. They are a finger food that is enjoyed by both adults and children! You can customize these bites by adding your favorite burger toppings. Try adding avocados or a slice of red onion. You can also swap out the Cheddar cheese for pepper jack cheese, American cheese, or even blue cheese as a tasty alternative.

Hands-On Time: 10 minutes
Cook Time: 6 minutes (per batch)

Serves 4

- 1 pound (93% lean) ground beef
- 1 tablespoon Worcestershire sauce
- 1 teaspoon salt
- 1 teaspoon dried oregano
- 1 teaspoon garlic powder
- ¼ teaspoon ground black pepper
- 5 (1-ounce) slices Cheddar cheese, quartered
- 6 leaves Bibb lettuce, torn into large pieces
- 1 pint cherry tomatoes
- 1 cup dill pickle chips

1 Preheat air fryer to 350°F.

2 In a large bowl, combine beef, Worcestershire, salt, oregano, garlic powder, and pepper. Mix well and form into twenty small patties.

3 Spray inside of air fryer with olive oil spray before each batch. Arrange patties inside air fryer so they are not touching (you may need to work in batches). Air fry 5 minutes. Patties will be done when they reach an internal temperature of 160°F.

4 Top patties with cheese and air fry an additional 1 minute or until melted.

5 Remove patties from air fryer and thread on skewers with lettuce, tomatoes, and pickles. Serve.

PER SERVING

CALORIES: 342 | **FAT:** 17g | **SODIUM:** 1,241mg | **CARBOHYDRATES:** 8g | **FIBER:** 2g | **SUGAR:** 4g | **PROTEIN:** 34g

4

Side Dishes

When thinking of comfort food, you might instantly think of the main course. However, comforting side dishes are just as important. Are hamburgers really as good without a serving of fries on the side? In this chapter, you will explore the many possible configurations of the potato side dish: Garlic Parmesan French Fries, Loaded Baked Potatoes, Sweet Potato Mash, and more. There are a wide variety of other side dish comfort food favorites like Green Bean Casserole, Hush Puppies, Mexican Street Corn, or Bacon-Stuffed Mushrooms. Find a new side dish to pair with your comfort food main dish of choice, or fill up your plate with side dishes only. The choice is yours, and either way it will be delicious!

Cheddar Bacon Broccoli

This broccoli dish is a comforting side dish that is ready to eat in just over 20 minutes. You can't beat the combination of bacon and melted cheese. It may even convince broccoli haters to change their minds. Frozen broccoli can be used in place of fresh broccoli. Simply prepare the broccoli from frozen and add 2 minutes to the initial cook time, before adding the cheese.

Hands-On Time: 10 minutes
Cook Time: 12 minutes

Serves 4

1 pound broccoli, cut into florets
3 tablespoons olive oil
1 teaspoon salt
1 cup shredded sharp Cheddar cheese
¼ cup crumbled cooked bacon

1 Preheat air fryer to 400°F.

2 In a large bowl, combine broccoli, olive oil, and salt. Toss to coat evenly.

3 Arrange broccoli inside air fryer. Air fry 10 minutes, shaking or turning halfway through.

4 Top cooked broccoli with cheese. Air fry an additional 2 minutes or until cheese is melted.

5 Remove from air fryer, sprinkle with bacon, and serve.

PER SERVING

CALORIES: 270 | **FAT:** 21g | **SODIUM:** 948mg | **CARBOHYDRATES:** 5g | **FIBER:** 2g | **SUGAR:** 1g | **PROTEIN:** 12g

Garlic Parmesan French Fries

Make your own garlic fries at home with this easy and delicious recipe! These fries are crispy on the outside and soft on the inside—plus they're coated with fresh garlic and loads of Parmesan cheese. Make sure to soak the potatoes; it makes all the difference in the texture of the fries.

Hands-On Time: 10 minutes
Cook Time: 16 minutes (per batch)

Serves 4

- 4 medium russet potatoes, cut into ¼"-thick strips
- 2 tablespoons olive oil
- ¼ cup grated Parmesan cheese
- 1 tablespoon minced garlic
- 1 teaspoon salt
- ¼ teaspoon garlic powder
- ¼ teaspoon ground black pepper

KEEPING FRIES WARM

When making fries in an air fryer, you will need to work in batches. Store cooked French fries in a warm oven until all fries have been cooked, or store them on a plate covered in a couple of layers of aluminum foil.

1 Fill a medium bowl with cold water and soak cut potatoes 1 hour, changing the water every 20 minutes.

2 Rinse and drain potatoes. Pat dry.

3 Preheat air fryer to 380°F.

4 In a large bowl, toss potatoes in oil, Parmesan, minced garlic, salt, garlic powder, and pepper.

5 Working in batches, arrange potatoes in an even layer inside air fryer. Air fry 16 minutes or until crispy, shaking or turning halfway through.

6 Remove from air fryer. Serve.

PER SERVING

CALORIES: 257 | FAT: 8g | SODIUM: 718mg | CARBOHYDRATES: 39g | FIBER: 4g | SUGAR: 2g | PROTEIN: 7g

Cheesy Bacon Fries

Want to make your homemade fries taste even better? Turn them into cheese fries! This recipe takes perfectly crisp homemade French fries and tops them with two types of melted cheese, smoky bacon, and sliced green onions. You really can't go wrong with French fries, and this variety tastes great on its own or served with the Herb and Cheese-Stuffed Burgers (see Chapter 6). If you're looking for dipping sauce inspiration, switch things up with ranch dressing or keep it classic with ketchup.

Hands-On Time: 10 minutes
Cook Time: 16 minutes (per batch plus 2 minutes to melt cheese)

Serves 4

- 4 medium russet potatoes, cut into ¼"-thick strips, keeping skin on
- 2 tablespoons olive oil
- 1 teaspoon salt
- 1 cup shredded Cheddar cheese
- ½ cup shredded mozzarella cheese
- ½ cup crumbled cooked bacon
- ⅛ cup finely sliced green onions

1 Fill a medium bowl with cold water and soak cut potatoes 1 hour, changing the water every 20 minutes.

2 Rinse and drain potatoes. Pat dry.

3 Preheat air fryer to 380°F.

4 In a large bowl, toss potatoes in olive oil and salt.

5 Working in batches, arrange potatoes in an even layer inside air fryer. Air fry 16 minutes or until crispy, shaking or turning halfway through.

6 Once all of the fries have been cooked, place them back in the air fryer and top with Cheddar cheese, mozzarella cheese, and bacon. Air fry 2 minutes or until cheese is melted.

7 Remove from air fryer, then top with green onions and serve.

PER SERVING

CALORIES: 461 | **FAT:** 23g | **SODIUM:** 1,185mg | **CARBOHYDRATES:** 39g | **FIBER:** 4g | **SUGAR:** 2g | **PROTEIN:** 21g

Green Beans with Bacon

This recipe calls for fresh green beans, but they can be substituted with two (15-ounce) cans of green beans. Drain the beans well and dry between two sheets of paper towels prior to cooking.

Hands-On Time: 10 minutes
Cook Time: 12 minutes

Serves 4

1 pound fresh green beans, trimmed
2 tablespoons olive oil
1 teaspoon salt
1 teaspoon garlic powder
½ teaspoon ground black pepper
1 large shallot, peeled and chopped
4 slices thick-cut bacon, chopped

1 Preheat air fryer to 370°F.

2 In a large bowl, toss green beans with olive oil, salt, garlic powder, and pepper.

3 Arrange green beans inside air fryer, then top with shallot and bacon.

4 Air fry 12 minutes, stirring halfway through.

5 Remove from air fryer. Serve.

PER SERVING

CALORIES: 204 | FAT: 14g | SODIUM: 975mg | CARBOHYDRATES: 9g | FIBER: 3g | SUGAR: 4g | PROTEIN: 10g

Sweet Potato Casserole

Say hello to your new favorite sweet and comforting side dish! Watch the dish carefully, as the marshmallows quickly melt in the air fryer and tend to burn if left unattended.

Hands-On Time: 10 minutes
Cook Time: 12 minutes

Serves 4

3 (15-ounce) cans sweet potatoes, drained
½ cup packed light brown sugar
¼ cup salted butter, melted
3 tablespoons orange juice
⅛ teaspoon ground cinnamon
1 (10-ounce) bag mini marshmallows

1 Preheat air fryer to 320°F. Spray a 7" 5" baking dish with olive oil spray and set aside.

2 In a large bowl, combine sweet potatoes, brown sugar, butter, orange juice, and cinnamon. Mix until fully combined. Spoon mixture into prepared baking dish.

3 Place baking dish inside air fryer and air fry 10 minutes. Top sweet potatoes with mini marshmallows and air fry an additional 2 minutes or until marshmallows are golden brown.

4 Remove dish from air fryer. Serve.

PER SERVING

CALORIES: 664 | FAT: 11g | SODIUM: 287mg | CARBOHYDRATES: 139g | FIBER: 5g | SUGAR: 81g | PROTEIN: 6g

Green Bean Casserole

Green Bean Casserole is a classic holiday side dish, and for good reason. It's a comforting casserole made of green beans and a creamy sauce, then topped with buttery crackers and sharp Cheddar cheese. This recipe can be prepared ahead of time and stored in the refrigerator for up to 2 days before cooking it in the air fryer.

Hands-On Time: 20 minutes
Cook Time: 14 minutes

Serves 4

2 (15-ounce) cans French-style green beans
1 (10.5-ounce) can cream of mushroom soup
½ cup whole milk
1 cup shredded sharp Cheddar cheese, divided
½ teaspoon salt
⅛ teaspoon ground black pepper
6 round butter crackers, crushed

USING FRESH GREEN BEANS

Fresh green beans may be used in this Green Bean Casserole recipe. Instead of the two cans of green beans, use 1 pound fresh green beans. Just trim the ends off the beans and continue the recipe.

1 Preheat air fryer to 350°F. Spray a 7" × 5" baking dish with olive oil spray and set aside.

2 In a large bowl, combine green beans, cream of mushroom soup, milk, ½ cup cheese, salt, and pepper. Mix well.

3 Pour green bean mixture into prepared dish and place dish inside air fryer. Air fry 12 minutes, stirring halfway through.

4 Top casserole with remaining ½ cup cheese and crushed crackers. Air fry an additional 2 minutes.

5 Remove dish from air fryer, then serve.

PER SERVING

CALORIES: 241 | **FAT:** 14g | **SODIUM:** 1,314mg | **CARBOHYDRATES:** 15g | **FIBER:** 3g | **SUGAR:** 3g | **PROTEIN:** 10g

Parmesan Asparagus

Asparagus cooks quickly in the air fryer, making it an easy side dish to whip up at the last minute. It's a healthy and crispy side that tastes great when paired with seafood or beef. Feel free to add additional Parmesan cheese to the asparagus once served. If you want to add a little something extra, serve with ranch dressing as a dipping sauce!

Hands-On Time: 5 minutes
Cook Time: 8 minutes

Serves 4

1 pound asparagus, trimmed
1 tablespoon olive oil
1 teaspoon garlic salt
¼ teaspoon ground black pepper
¼ cup grated Parmesan cheese

CHOOSING ASPARAGUS

This recipe was written for asparagus that's thicker, about ½" thick. If you are cooking thinner asparagus, then cut the cook time down to 6 minutes and monitor it as it cooks.

1   Preheat air fryer to 400°F.

2   In a large bowl, toss asparagus with olive oil, garlic salt, and pepper. Arrange inside air fryer, then sprinkle with Parmesan cheese.

3   Air fry 8 minutes or until fork-tender.

4   Remove from air fryer and serve immediately.

PER SERVING

CALORIES: 68 | FAT: 5g | SODIUM: 604mg | CARBOHYDRATES: 3g | FIBER: 1g | SUGAR: 1g | PROTEIN: 3g

Broccoli Casserole

Broccoli Casserole is a rich and decadent side dish. Softened broccoli coated with melted cheese and topped with crunchy butter crackers makes a dish not soon forgotten. It's often served during the holidays but can be enjoyed at any time of year—especially since this air fryer version is ready in under 30 minutes.

Hands-On Time: 20 minutes
Cook Time: 18 minutes

Serves 4

- 1 pound broccoli, cut into florets
- 3 tablespoons olive oil
- 1 teaspoon salt
- 8 ounces cream cheese, softened
- 1 cup shredded Cheddar cheese
- 6 round butter crackers, crushed

1 Preheat air fryer to 400°F. Spray a 7" 5" baking dish with olive oil spray and set aside.

2 In a large bowl, combine broccoli, olive oil, and salt. Toss to coat evenly. Then place broccoli inside air fryer.

3 Air fry 5 minutes, shaking or turning halfway through.

4 Place cooked broccoli in a clean large bowl. Add cream cheese and Cheddar cheese. Mix well. Pour broccoli mixture into prepared baking dish and cover with foil.

5 Place dish inside air fryer. Air fry 10 minutes. Remove foil from dish and top broccoli mixture with crushed crackers, then air fry an additional 3 minutes.

6 Remove dish from air fryer. Serve.

PER SERVING

CALORIES: 445 | **FAT:** 36g | **SODIUM:** 1,036mg | **CARBOHYDRATES:** 10g | **FIBER:** 2g | **SUGAR:** 3g | **PROTEIN:** 12g

Loaded Baked Potatoes

These Loaded Baked Potatoes come out with crispy skin while being fork-tender on the inside! This recipe makes four baked potatoes that are topped with sour cream, Cheddar cheese, green onions, and bacon. If you want to serve chili potatoes, top them with chili, Cheddar cheese, green onions, and sour cream.

Hands-On Time: 10 minutes
Cook Time: 40 minutes

Serves 4

- 4 medium russet potatoes
- ¼ cup olive oil
- ½ teaspoon salt
- ¼ teaspoon ground black pepper
- ½ cup sour cream
- ¼ cup shredded sharp Cheddar cheese
- ¼ cup crumbled cooked bacon
- 2 green onions, sliced

POTATO COOKING TIMES

Depending on the size of your potato and strength of your air fryer, potatoes may need to be cooked for a little less or more time. The best way to test a potato for doneness is with the fork test. Simply slide the tines of a fork into the top of your potato. If it is done, they should slide in easily. If it takes some effort, continue cooking the potato for a few more minutes and try again.

1 Preheat air fryer to 400°F.

2 Prick potatoes all over with the tines of a fork. Rub olive oil over each potato and season with salt and pepper.

3 Place potatoes inside air fryer in a single layer. Air fry 30 minutes, then carefully flip potatoes over and air fry an additional 10 minutes.

4 Remove potatoes from air fryer and let sit 10 minutes. Cut the top of each potato lengthwise, then carefully pull the sides apart without cutting the potato completely in half. Top each potato with sour cream, cheese, bacon, and green onions. Serve immediately.

PER SERVING

CALORIES: 416 | **FAT:** 23g | **SODIUM:** 536mg | **CARBOHYDRATES:** 39g | **FIBER:** 4g | **SUGAR:** 3g | **PROTEIN:** 11g

Maple Cinnamon Sweet Potatoes

These sweet potatoes come out cooked to perfection and are topped with a delicious combination of maple syrup, ground cinnamon, and just a hint of cayenne pepper. The sweet potatoes are very fluffy in the center yet have crispy skin. When shopping for sweet potatoes, look for potatoes that don't have any wrinkles, soft spots, or cracks. They should be firm to the touch, not overly soft.

Hands-On Time: 20 minutes
Cook Time: 40 minutes

Serves 4

4 medium sweet potatoes
¼ cup olive oil
½ teaspoon salt
¼ teaspoon ground black pepper
¼ cup pure maple syrup
2 teaspoons ground cinnamon
¼ teaspoon cayenne pepper

1 Preheat air fryer to 400°F.

2 Prick sweet potatoes all over with the tines of a fork. Rub olive oil over each potato and season with salt and black pepper.

3 Place sweet potatoes inside air fryer in a single layer. Air fry 30 minutes, then carefully flip potatoes over and air fry an additional 10 minutes or until soft and fork-tender.

4 In a small bowl, whisk together maple syrup, cinnamon, and cayenne pepper. Set aside.

5 Remove sweet potatoes from air fryer and let sit 10 minutes. Cut the top of each potato lengthwise, then carefully pull the sides apart without cutting the potato completely in half. Drizzle maple syrup mixture over sweet potatoes and serve.

PER SERVING

CALORIES: 285 | FAT: 13g | SODIUM: 364mg | CARBOHYDRATES: 41g | FIBER: 5g | SUGAR: 17g | PROTEIN: 2g

Garlic Mushrooms

Garlic Mushrooms make a great side dish, or even can be a vegetarian main dish if you replace the Worcestershire sauce with a vegetarian-friendly alternative like soy sauce.

Hands-On Time: 10 minutes
Cook Time: 10 minutes

Serves 4

1 (8-ounce) package button mushrooms, halved
1 tablespoon olive oil
1 tablespoon lemon juice
1 teaspoon Worcestershire sauce
1 tablespoon chopped flat-leaf Italian parsley
1 teaspoon garlic powder
1 teaspoon salt
¼ teaspoon ground black pepper

1 Preheat air fryer to 400°F.

2 In a medium bowl, mix together mushrooms, olive oil, lemon juice, and Worcestershire sauce. Sprinkle with parsley, garlic powder, salt, and pepper. Mix again.

3 Place prepared mushrooms inside air fryer. Air fry 10 minutes, shaking or turning halfway through.

4 Remove from air fryer. Serve.

PER SERVING

CALORIES. 46 | FAT: 3g | SODIUM: 598mg | CARBOHYDRATES: 3g | FIBER: 1g | SUGAR: 1g | PROTEIN: 2g

Sweet Potato Mash

This mash tastes great any time of year, but especially in autumn months.

Hands-On Time: 20 minutes
Cook Time: 40 minutes

Serves 4

4 medium sweet potatoes
¼ cup olive oil
½ teaspoon salt
¼ teaspoon ground black pepper
½ cup salted butter, softened
½ cup whole milk

1 Preheat air fryer to 400°F.

2 Prick sweet potatoes all over with the tines of a fork. Rub olive oil over each potato and season with salt and pepper.

3 Place sweet potatoes inside air fryer. Air fry 30 minutes. Carefully flip potatoes over and air fry an additional 10 minutes or until soft. Remove sweet potatoes and let them cool slightly.

4 Remove skins from sweet potatoes and discard. In a large bowl, place potatoes and butter. Whisk until sweet potatoes are smooth and fluffy. Slowly add in milk, whisking the entire time. Serve.

PER SERVING

CALORIES: 443 | FAT: 36g | SODIUM: 527mg | CARBOHYDRATES: 25g | FIBER: 4g | SUGAR: 9g | PROTEIN: 4g

Mexican Street Corn

Mexican Street Corn, also known as *elotes*, is crispy corn on the cob slathered in a creamy combination of sour cream, cotija cheese, and mayonnaise. It's then sprinkled with chili powder, cilantro, and extra cotija cheese. The result is tender corn on the cob that's both spicy and citrusy. If you can find it, crema (Mexican sour cream) is excellent in the sauce. Otherwise, regular sour cream will also work.

Hands-On Time: 20 minutes
Cook Time: 10 minutes

Serves 4

- 4 medium ears corn, husks removed
- 2 tablespoons salted butter, melted
- ½ cup cotija cheese, crumbled and divided
- ¼ cup crema
- ¼ cup mayonnaise
- 1 medium lime, zested and juiced
- 2 tablespoons minced garlic
- ½ teaspoon salt
- 1 teaspoon chili powder
- ¼ cup finely chopped cilantro

1 Preheat air fryer to 400°F.

2 Brush butter on corn and place inside air fryer. Air fry 10 minutes, flipping halfway through.

3 In a medium bowl, combine ¼ cup cotija cheese, crema, mayonnaise, lime juice and zest, garlic, and salt. Mix well.

4 Remove corn from air fryer. Spread sauce on cooked corn. Sprinkle with chili powder, remaining 1/4 cup cotija cheese, and cilantro. Serve.

PER SERVING

CALORIES: 342 | FAT: 25g | SODIUM: 683mg | CARBOHYDRATES: 23g | FIBER: 2g | SUGAR: 7g | PROTEIN: 7g

Breaded Summer Squash

Enjoy one of summer's most plentiful vegetables with this crispy vegetable "chip" recipe. The summer squash comes out warm and tender, while the panko coating is perfectly crunchy and flavored with Parmesan cheese. You can serve the "chips" plain or with a side of ranch dressing for dipping. This recipe also works really well with zucchini!

Hands-On Time: 15 minutes
Cook Time: 10 minutes (per batch)

Serves 4

½ cup all-purpose flour
1 teaspoon Italian seasoning
1 teaspoon paprika
2 large eggs, beaten
2 cups panko bread crumbs
¼ cup grated Parmesan cheese
1 teaspoon garlic powder
1 teaspoon salt
¼ teaspoon ground black pepper
1 large summer squash, sliced into ¼"-thick rounds

1 Preheat air fryer to 400°F.

2 In a medium shallow bowl, place flour and mix in Italian seasoning and paprika. In another medium shallow bowl, place eggs. In a third medium shallow bowl, place bread crumbs and mix in Parmesan, garlic powder, salt, and pepper.

3 Dredge squash in flour mixture, turning to coat. Then dip squash in eggs, shaking to remove any excess. Finally, dip squash in bread crumb mixture, turning to evenly coat.

4 Spray inside of air fryer with olive oil spray before each batch. Arrange squash in a single layer inside air fryer (you may need to work in batches). Air fry 10 minutes, flipping halfway through.

5 Remove from air fryer. Serve.

PER SERVING

CALORIES: 172 | FAT: 3g | SODIUM: 130mg | CARBOHYDRATES: 29g | FIBER: 1g | SUGAR: 3g | PROTEIN: 8g

Herbed Red Potatoes

You are going to love this comforting and versatile side dish. This recipe uses baby red potatoes and coats them in olive oil, garlic, and lots of seasonings! They are air fried and then drizzled with a mouthwatering combination of melted butter and fresh parsley. If you can't get your hands on baby red potatoes, large red potatoes cut into 2" chunks may be substituted. Serve this with Lemon Butter Halibut (see Chapter 7) or Stuffed Pork Chops (see Chapter 6).

Hands-On Time: 15 minutes
Cook Time: 20 minutes

Serves 4

- 2 pounds baby red potatoes, halved
- 4 tablespoons olive oil
- 1 tablespoon garlic powder
- 1 teaspoon Italian seasoning
- 1 teaspoon salt
- ¼ teaspoon ground black pepper
- 3 tablespoons salted butter, melted
- 1 teaspoon chopped fresh flatleaf Italian parsley

1   Preheat air fryer to 400°F.

2   In a large bowl, combine potatoes, olive oil, garlic powder, Italian seasoning, salt, and pepper. Mix well.

3   Arrange prepared potatoes inside air fryer. Air fry 20 minutes (shaking or turning halfway through) or until golden brown.

4   Remove potatoes from air fryer. Whisk together melted butter and parsley, then pour herb butter over potatoes and serve.

PER SERVING

CALORIES: 362 | FAT: 21g | SODIUM: 692mg | CARBOHYDRATES: 38g | FIBER: 4g | SUGAR: 3g | PROTEIN: 5g

Hush Puppies

Hush Puppies are delicious, onion-flavored cornmeal fritters. They come out crispy on the outside and chewy on the inside. To store leftover Hush Puppies, let them cool completely and then store in an airtight container in the refrigerator for up to 3 days. Serve them with Honey Garlic Shrimp (see Chapter 7) for a nice contrast in flavor.

Hands-On Time: 20 minutes
Cook Time: 10 minutes (per batch)

Serves 6 (2 fritters each)

1 cup yellow cornmeal
¾ cup all-purpose flour
½ small yellow onion, peeled and diced
1½ teaspoons baking powder
¾ teaspoon salt
½ teaspoon garlic powder
½ teaspoon onion powder
1 large egg
¾ cup buttermilk
2 tablespoons olive oil

1 Preheat air fryer to 400°F.

2 In a large bowl, combine cornmeal, flour, onion, baking powder, salt, garlic powder, and onion powder. Whisk in egg and buttermilk. Let rest 5 minutes.

3 Separate dough into twelve pieces and roll each piece into a ball. Brush each ball of dough with olive oil.

4 Arrange dough balls inside air fryer, spaced 1" apart (you may need to work in batches). Air fry 10 minutes or until golden brown, flipping halfway through.

5 Remove from air fryer. Serve.

PER SERVING

CALORIES: 205 | FAT: 7g | SODIUM: 463mg | CARBOHYDRATES: 30g | FIBER: 2g | SUGAR: 2g | PROTEIN: 5g

Garlic Zucchini

This recipe is flavored simply with garlic powder, salt, pepper, and Parmesan cheese. Garlic Zucchini pairs nicely with whitefish like the Italian Butter Cod (see Chapter 7).

Hands-On Time: 10 minutes
Cook Time: 10 minutes

Serves 4

1 pound zucchini, cut into 1" rounds
1 teaspoon garlic powder
½ teaspoon salt
¼ teaspoon ground black pepper
¼ cup grated Parmesan cheese

1 Preheat air fryer to 400°F.

2 Season zucchini with garlic powder, salt, and pepper.

3 Arrange seasoned zucchini inside air fryer in a single layer. Top each round with Parmesan cheese. Air fry 10 minutes or until cheese is golden brown.

4 Remove from air fryer and serve.

PER SERVING

CALORIES: 47 | FAT. 2g | SODIUM: 412mg | CARBOHYDRATES: 5g | FIBER: 1g | SUGAR: 3g | PROTEIN: 3g

Broccoli and Garlic

If you want to make this side dish extra special, try sprinkling it with some fresh grated Parmesan cheese right before serving it. This side dish is extremely versatile but tastes great paired with Rib Eye Steak (see Chapter 6).

Hands-On Time: 15 minutes
Cook Time: 12 minutes

Serves 4

1 pound broccoli, cut into florets
1 head garlic, cloves separated and peeled
3 tablespoons olive oil
1 teaspoon salt
¼ teaspoon ground black pepper

1 Preheat air fryer to 400°F

2 In a large bowl, combine all ingredients. Toss to coat evenly.

3 Place broccoli inside air fryer. Air fry 12 minutes, shaking or turning halfway through.

4 Remove from air fryer. Serve.

PER SERVING

CALORIES: 126 | FAT: 10g | SODIUM: 605mg | CARBOHYDRATES: 8g | FIBER: 2g | SUGAR: 1g | PROTEIN: 3g

Garlic Parmesan Carrot Fries

Carrot fries are a fun alternative to boiled or roasted carrots. They come out extra crispy with a tender center. The garlic and Parmesan make the carrots feel more "fry"-like and add a depth of flavor. Serve these carrot fries on their own or with a side of ranch dressing for dipping. Cooled carrot fries can be stored in the refrigerator for up to 3 days and reheated in the air fryer for 3-5 minutes at 300°F.

Hands-On Time: 10 minutes
Cook Time: 16 minutes

Serves 4

- 1 pound carrots, peeled and sliced into 2" × ¼" wedges
- 2 tablespoons olive oil
- 1 teaspoon minced garlic
- ½ teaspoon garlic salt
- ¼ teaspoon ground black pepper
- ¼ cup grated Parmesan cheese

1 Preheat air fryer to 350°F.

2 In a medium bowl, combine all ingredients except cheese. Toss to coat evenly.

3 Arrange carrots inside air fryer in a single layer. Air fry 15 minutes, shaking or turning halfway through. Sprinkle Parmesan cheese over carrots and air fry 1 additional minute or until cheese is golden brown.

4 Remove from air fryer and serve.

PER SERVING

CALORIES: 132 | FAT: 8g | SODIUM: 433mg | CARBOHYDRATES: 12g | FIBER: 3g | SUGAR: 5g | PROTEIN: 3g

Crispy Okra

This breaded, perfectly seasoned okra is a comforting side dish. It comes out of the air fryer a perfect golden brown and brimming with flavor in just 10 minutes. Serve with Pork Tenderloin Medallions (see Chapter 6) for a delicious, hearty meal.

Hands-On Time: 10 minutes
Cook Time: 10 minutes

Serves 4

⅓ cup buttermilk
½ cup cornmeal
½ cup all-purpose flour
½ teaspoon garlic powder
½ teaspoon paprika
½ teaspoon salt
¼ teaspoon ground black pepper
1 pound okra, cut into ½" slices

KEEP OKRA FROM GETTING SLIMY

When preparing the okra, rinse it instead of soaking it. Then dry it well and quickly. To truly cut down on the sliminess, slice okra into slightly large pieces. Aim for ½" slices.

1 Preheat air fryer to 400°F.

2 Pour buttermilk in a medium bowl. In another medium bowl, place cornmeal, flour, garlic powder, paprika, salt, and pepper and stir to combine. Dip each piece of okra in buttermilk and then roll in cornmeal mixture.

3 Spray inside of air fryer with olive oil spray and arrange okra inside air fryer in an even layer. Spray okra with olive oil spray. Air fry 10 minutes, stirring halfway through or until okra is golden brown.

4 Remove from air fryer and serve.

PER SERVING

CALORIES: 155 | FAT: 1g | SODIUM: 323mg | CARBOHYDRATES: 32g | FIBER: 5g | SUGAR: 2g | PROTEIN: 5g

Bacon-Stuffed Mushrooms

Stuffed mushrooms are an indulgent treat! This version features tender button mushrooms stuffed with a tantalizing combination of bacon, Parmesan cheese, and cream cheese. These mushrooms are air fried until the cheese is crispy while the inside stays juicy and tender. They are topped with sliced green onion for a layer of freshness. Baby bella mushrooms can also be used.

Hands-On Time: 15 minutes
Cook Time: 8 minutes (per batch)

Serves 4

- ½ pound button mushrooms, stems removed and reserved
- ¼ cup grated Parmesan cheese, divided
- 4 ounces cream cheese, softened
- 1 teaspoon minced garlic
- ½ teaspoon salt
- 4 slices bacon, cooked and crumbled
- 1 green onion, thinly sliced

1 Preheat air fryer to 390°F.

2 In the bowl of a food processor, combine mushroom stems, ⅛ cup Parmesan cheese, cream cheese, garlic, and salt. Process until finely chopped, about 20 seconds. Fold in bacon.

3 Use a spoon to fill each mushroom cap with prepared filling. Sprinkle top of each filled mushroom with remaining 1/8 cup Parmesan cheese.

4 Working in batches, carefully place stuffed mushrooms inside air fryer in a single layer. Spray top of each mushroom with olive oil spray. Air fry 8 minutes or until tender and golden brown.

5 Remove mushrooms from air fryer, top with sliced green onion, and serve.

PER SERVING

CALORIES: 180 | FAT: 12g | SODIUM: 672mg | CARBOHYDRATES: 4g | FIBER: 1g | SUGAR: 2g | PROTEIN: 9g

5

Chicken Main Dishes

Say goodbye to boring baked chicken! In the air fryer, you can make delicious juicy chicken in under 30 minutes. This chapter covers classic comfort food chicken dishes like Chicken Parmesan, Southern Fried Chicken, and Chicken Nuggets. You will also learn how to get creative with your chicken and turn it into meals like Fajita-Stuffed Chicken and Chicken Kebabs. Want a takeout-inspired chicken dish? Try making Popcorn Chicken or Sweet and Sour Chicken. You can't go wrong with any of these comforting chicken dishes!

Teriyaki Chicken

This Teriyaki Chicken dish is a wonderfully simple comfort food, yet extremely flavorful thanks to the flavor-packed homemade teriyaki marinade. The chicken thighs stay extra juicy when cooked in the air fryer. Serve this with a side of sticky rice and grilled pineapple.

Hands-On Time: 10 minutes
Cook Time: 18 minutes

Serves 4

½ cup low-sodium soy sauce
½ cup rice vinegar
½ cup packed light brown sugar
1 tablespoon cornstarch
1 teaspoon minced ginger
¼ teaspoon garlic powder
8 boneless, skinless chicken thighs (1 pound total)

1 In a small bowl, mix together soy sauce, rice vinegar, brown sugar, cornstarch, ginger, and garlic powder.

2 Place chicken in a medium shallow dish and pour teriyaki sauce over chicken. Refrigerate a minimum of 20 minutes.

3 Preheat air fryer to 400°F.

4 Remove chicken from marinade and arrange in a single layer inside air fryer. Air fry 18 minutes, flipping chicken halfway through. Chicken is done when it reaches an internal temperature of 165°F.

5 Remove from air fryer. Serve.

PER SERVING

CALORIES: 394 | **FAT:** 16g | **SODIUM:** 254mg | **CARBOHYDRATES:** 1g | **FIBER:** 0g | **SUGAR:** 0g | **PROTEIN:** 55g

Nashville Hot Chicken

This Southern chicken is savory, spicy, and just a little bit sweet. It's served on a hamburger bun and topped with sliced dill pickles. The combination of sweet and spicy makes this chicken sandwich anything but boring! Serve it with Cheesy Bacon Fries (see Chapter 4).

Hands-On Time: 20 minutes
Cook Time: 18 minutes

Serves 4

- 1½ cups buttermilk
- 2 tablespoons hot sauce
- 2 tablespoons dill pickle juice
- 1 large egg, lightly beaten
- 2 teaspoons salt, divided
- 4 boneless, skinless chicken breasts (1 pound total)
- 1½ cups all-purpose flour
- ½ cup cornstarch
- ½ teaspoon ground black pepper
- 4 tablespoons vegetable oil
- 2 tablespoons unsalted butter, melted
- 2 tablespoons cayenne pepper
- 1 tablespoon packed light brown sugar
- 1 teaspoon paprika
- 4 hamburger buns
- 1 whole dill pickle, sliced

NASHVILLE HOT CHICKEN ORIGIN

If the rumors are true, the original Nashville Hot Chicken was created by a woman who wanted to teach her cheating boyfriend a lesson. She served him his favorite dish—fried chicken—coated in hot sauce.

1 In a medium shallow dish, mix together buttermilk, hot sauce, pickle juice, egg, and 1 teaspoon salt. Place chicken in dish and turn to coat. Refrigerate a minimum of 20 minutes.

2 Preheat air fryer to 400°F.

3 In a medium shallow bowl, mix together flour, cornstarch, remaining 1 teaspoon salt, and black pepper.

4 Remove chicken from buttermilk. Dredge chicken in flour mixture, turning to coat.

5 Spray inside of air fryer with olive oil spray. Place chicken inside air fryer and spray top of chicken with olive oil spray. Air fry 18 minutes, flipping halfway through. Chicken is done when it reaches an internal temperature of 165°F.

6 In a small bowl, mix together vegetable oil, butter, cayenne pepper, brown sugar, and paprika. Remove chicken from air fryer and brush both sides of chicken with sauce. Divide chicken among 4 buns and top with sliced pickles. Serve.

PER SERVING

CALORIES: 529 | **FAT:** 25g | **SODIUM:** 938mg | **CARBOHYDRATES:** 41g | **FIBER:** 3g | **SUGAR:** 8g | **PROTEIN:** 34g

Fajita-Stuffed Chicken

This chicken dish is all of the flavors you love from chicken fajitas, stuffed inside crispy and juicy air fryer chicken. The bell peppers and onion come out tender, while the chicken is seasoned perfectly and topped with lime juice and cilantro.

Hands-On Time: 15 minutes
Cook Time: 26 minutes

Serves 4

1 tablespoon olive oil
2 large white mushrooms, diced
1 large red bell pepper, seeded and diced
½ small white onion, peeled and diced
1 tablespoon minced garlic
4 boneless, skinless chicken breasts (1 pound total)
1 tablespoon taco seasoning
2 tablespoons lime juice
2 tablespoons chopped fresh cilantro

1 In a large skillet, heat olive oil over medium-high heat. Add mushrooms, bell pepper, and onion. Cook, stirring occasionally, until soft, about 7 minutes. Mix in garlic and cook an additional 1 minute or until fragrant. Remove from heat and set aside.

2 Preheat air fryer to 400°F.

3 Butterfly chicken breasts and rub outside of chicken with taco seasoning. Fill the center of each chicken breast with vegetable mixture, close chicken breasts, and secure with toothpicks.

4 Spray inside of air fryer with olive oil spray. Arrange chicken inside air fryer in a single layer. Air fry 18 minutes, flipping halfway through. Chicken is done when it reaches an internal temperature of 165°F.

5 Remove chicken from air fryer and remove toothpicks. Top each piece of chicken with lime juice and cilantro, then serve.

PER SERVING

CALORIES: 182 | FAT: 6g | SODIUM: 198mg | CARBOHYDRATES: 6g | FIBER: 1g | SUGAR: 3g | PROTEIN: 26g

Pesto-Stuffed Chicken

In this dish, juicy chicken is stuffed with a combination of bright, herby pesto and sweet-tart sun-dried tomatoes. The chicken is then topped with a combination of Parmesan and mozzarella cheeses to make this dish both rich and comforting. For best results, start with blocks of fresh Parmesan and mozzarella cheeses and grate them yourself. This will guarantee smooth, perfectly melted cheese.

Hands-On Time: 15 minutes
Cook Time: 18 minutes

Serves 4

- 4 boneless, skinless chicken breasts (1 pound total)
- 1 teaspoon salt
- 1 teaspoon garlic powder
- ½ teaspoon ground black pepper
- 1 cup basil pesto
- 1 cup shredded mozzarella cheese, divided
- ½ cup sun-dried tomatoes, finely chopped
- ½ cup grated Parmesan cheese

HOMEMADE PESTO
Purée 1 cup fresh basil, 3 cloves garlic, 3 tablespoons pine nuts, and ⅓ cup grated Parmesan. Slowly pour in ¼ cup olive oil while puréeing and season to taste.

1. Preheat air fryer to 400°F.

2. Place chicken between two pieces of plastic wrap or parchment paper. Using a meat tenderizer, lightly pound chicken until ¼" thick throughout. Season both sides of chicken with salt, garlic powder, and pepper.

3. In a medium bowl, mix together pesto, ¼ cup mozzarella cheese, and sun-dried tomatoes. Spread pesto mixture in center of each piece of chicken. Roll up chicken lengthwise and secure with toothpicks.

4. Spray inside of air fryer with olive oil spray. Place chicken inside air fryer and air fry 15 minutes. Sprinkle remaining ¾ cup mozzarella and Parmesan over chicken. Air fry an additional 3 minutes. Chicken is done when it reaches an internal temperature of 165°F.

5. Remove chicken from air fryer, remove toothpicks from chicken (leaving the chicken rolled), and cut chicken into 1" slices. Serve.

PER SERVING

CALORIES: 566 | FAT: 36g | SODIUM: 1,718mg | CARBOHYDRATES: 15g | FIBER: 2g | SUGAR: 6g | PROTEIN: 43g

Buffalo Chicken Taquitos

This spicy take on chicken taquitos is made with a tasty homemade buffalo sauce. Choose your favorite hot sauce when making this recipe. Keep in mind that the spicier the hot sauce, the spicier the taquitos will be. You can use blue cheese dressing instead of ranch for a dipping sauce, if you prefer, or you can enjoy the taquitos plain. They can be cooled after cooking and frozen for up to 3 months. To reheat, warm in the air fryer at 350°F for about 5 minutes.

Hands-On Time: 25 minutes

Cook Time: 5 minutes (per batch)

Serves 4

- 1½ cups hot sauce
- 4 tablespoons unsalted butter, melted
- 2 tablespoons Worcestershire sauce
- 1 tablespoon red wine vinegar
- 2½ cups shredded cooked chicken
- 12 (6") corn tortillas
- ½ cup ranch dressing

1 Preheat air fryer to 400°F.

2 In a medium bowl, mix together hot sauce, butter, Worcestershire sauce, and vinegar. Add chicken and stir to evenly coat.

3 Fill each tortilla with ⅛ cup chicken mixture, roll up tightly, and secure with a toothpick.

4 Arrange taquitos inside air fryer, spaced ½" apart. Spray with olive oil spray. Air fry 5 minutes or until crispy. Work in batches if needed, spraying inside of air fryer with olive oil spray each time.

5 Remove taquitos from air fryer, remove toothpicks, and serve taquitos with ranch dressing on the side.

PER SERVING

CALORIES: 417 | FAT: 16g | SODIUM: 2,958mg | CARBOHYDRATES: 34g | FIBER: 5g | SUGAR: 2g | PROTEIN: 31g

Chicken Caprese

This chicken dish is inspired by the traditional salad. The chicken is complemented by the juiciness of the tomatoes and saltiness and creaminess of the mozzarella. Serve with Garlic Zucchini (see Chapter 4) for a filling and appetizing meal.

Hands-On Time: 10 minutes
Cook Time: 18 minutes

Serves 4

- 4 tablespoons olive oil
- 4 boneless, skinless chicken breasts (1 pound total)
- ½ teaspoon salt
- ¼ teaspoon ground black pepper
- ¼ teaspoon dried oregano
- 6 ounces mozzarella cheese, sliced ¼" thick
- 3 large tomatoes, sliced ½" thick
- ¼ cup chopped fresh basil

1 Preheat air fryer to 380°F.

2 Brush olive oil on both sides of chicken and sprinkle with salt, pepper, and oregano.

3 Place chicken inside air fryer in a single layer and air fry 10 minutes. Flip chicken over and top with mozzarella cheese. Air fry an additional 8 minutes. Chicken is done when it reaches an internal temperature of 165°F.

4 Remove chicken from air fryer. Arrange tomato and basil over chicken and serve.

PER SERVING

CALORIES: 396 | FAT: 23g | SODIUM: 629mg | CARBOHYDRATES: 9g | FIBER: 2g | SUGAR: 5g | PROTEIN: 36g

CAPRESE SALAD

The salad that inspired this dish is made with a combination of sliced tomatoes, sliced mozzarella, and fresh basil leaves. It's then seasoned with salt and pepper and drizzled with olive oil.

Salsa Chicken Casserole

This spicy and filling casserole comes out crispy on top yet moist on the inside. This chicken casserole tastes great when served with sour cream, guacamole, and black olives. Or you can top it with your favorite taco toppings. Prepare it ahead of time and store in the refrigerator for up to 24 hours prior to cooking for a low-effort meal when you get home.

Hands-On Time: 10 minutes
Cook Time: 20 minutes

Serves 4

2 cups shredded cooked chicken
1 cup salsa verde
½ cup sour cream
1½ cups shredded Mexican cheese blend, divided
2 teaspoons taco seasoning
6 (6") corn tortillas

HOMEMADE TACO SEASONING
Mix together your own taco seasoning with 1 tablespoon chili powder, 1½ teaspoons cumin, 1 teaspoon salt, 1 teaspoon ground black pepper, ½ teaspoon paprika, ¼ teaspoon garlic powder, ¼ teaspoon onion powder, ¼ teaspoon crushed red pepper flakes, and ¼ teaspoon dried oregano.

1 Preheat air fryer to 375°F. Spray a 7" cake pan with olive oil spray and set aside.

2 In a large bowl, combine chicken, salsa verde, sour cream, ½ cup cheese, and taco seasoning. Mix well.

3 Arrange 3 tortillas in prepared cake pan, sightly overlapping, so they fully cover the bottom. Spread half of chicken mixture over tortillas and top with remaining 3 tortillas. Top tortillas with remaining chicken mixture. Top chicken with remaining 1 cup cheese.

4 Place prepared casserole inside air fryer and air fry 20 minutes.

5 Remove pan from air fryer. Serve.

PER SERVING

CALORIES: 433 | **FAT:** 19g | **SODIUM:** 785mg | **CARBOHYDRATES:** 22g | **FIBER:** 2g | **SUGAR:** 6g | **PROTEIN:** 34g

Spiced Chicken Leg Quarters

This recipe is very easy to prepare and tastes great as leftovers too. Serve with rice and a side of Green Beans with Bacon (see Chapter 4).

Hands-On Time: 15 minutes
Cook Time: 25 minutes

Serves 4

2 tablespoons olive oil
1 teaspoon paprika
1 teaspoon salt
½ teaspoon ground black pepper
½ teaspoon onion powder
½ teaspoon garlic powder
¼ teaspoon ground mustard
¼ teaspoon cayenne pepper
4 chicken leg quarters, bone-in, skin-on (1½ pounds total)

1 Preheat air fryer to 380°F.

2 In a small bowl, whisk together olive oil, paprika, salt, black pepper, onion powder, garlic powder, ground mustard, and cayenne pepper. Brush oil mixture all over chicken.

3 Place chicken inside air fryer and air fry 25 minutes. Chicken is done when it reaches an internal temperature of 165°F.

4 Remove from air fryer. Serve.

PER SERVING

CALORIES: 489 | FAT: 21g | SODIUM: 834mg | CARBOHYDRATES: 1g | FIBER: 0g | SUGAR: 0g | PROTEIN: 62g

Pineapple Chicken

This Pineapple Chicken is a tasty blend of sweet and spicy. Serve it with white rice and macaroni salad.

Hands-On Time: 10 minutes
Cook Time: 18 minutes

Serves 4

1 (20-ounce) can crushed pineapple
1 (18-ounce) bottle sweet barbecue sauce
1 tablespoon red pepper flakes
4 boneless, skinless chicken breasts (1 pound total)

1 In a large bowl, combine pineapple, barbecue sauce, and red pepper flakes. Add chicken, stir to coat, and cover bowl with plastic wrap. Place bowl in refrigerator and let chicken marinate a minimum of 20 minutes or up to 24 hours.

2 Preheat air fryer to 380°F. Drain marinade and place chicken inside air fryer in a single layer. Air fry 18 minutes, flipping halfway through. Chicken is done when it reaches an internal temperature of 165°F.

3 Remove from air fryer. Serve.

PER SERVING

CALORIES: 145 | FAT: 2g | SODIUM: 173mg | CARBOHYDRATES: 5g | FIBER: 0g | SUGAR: 4g | PROTEIN: 25g

Sweet and Sour Chicken

This chicken is the perfect combination of sweet and sour ingredients. The dish is not spicy; however, it does have a bit of tangy flavor thanks to the apple cider vinegar. The sauce comes out sticky and coats the chicken perfectly. Sweet and Sour Chicken is best served with sticky white rice or fried rice. To reheat leftover chicken, air fry in the air fryer 2–3 minutes at 390°F.

Hands-On Time: 20 minutes

Cook Time: 16 minutes (per batch, plus 10 minutes on stove)

Serves 4

- 2 pounds boneless, skinless chicken breasts, cut into 1" chunks
- 1 cup cornstarch
- 1 cup apple cider vinegar
- 1 cup granulated sugar
- ½ cup ketchup
- 2 tablespoons low-sodium soy sauce
- 1½ teaspoons garlic powder
- ½ teaspoon salt
- ¼ teaspoon ground black pepper

1 Preheat air fryer to 380°F.

2 In a large bowl, combine chicken and cornstarch and toss chicken to evenly coat.

3 Spray inside of air fryer with olive oil spray. Arrange chicken inside air fryer in a single layer. Work in batches if needed, spraying inside of air fryer with olive oil spray each time. Spray top of chicken with olive oil spray. Air fry 16 minutes, flipping halfway through. Chicken is done when it reaches an internal temperature of 165°F.

4 In a medium saucepan over medium-high heat, combine apple cider vinegar, sugar, ketchup, soy sauce, garlic powder, salt, and pepper. Bring to a boil, stirring constantly. Reduce heat to low and let simmer 10 minutes.

5 Remove chicken from air fryer and pour sauce over chicken. Serve.

PER SERVING

CALORIES: 544 | FAT: 5g | SODIUM: 869mg | CARBOHYDRATES: 75g | FIBER: 0g | SUGAR: 57g / PROTEIN: 51g

Buffalo Chicken Tenders

A delicious combination of ingredients makes the perfect buttery, tangy, and spicy buffalo sauce for these chicken tenders. Serve this chicken dish with blue cheese dressing on the side for dipping, along with some fresh crunchy vegetables like celery and carrot sticks. These are sure to be a hit at your next sporting event viewing party!

Hands-On Time: 20 minutes
Cook Time: 21 minutes

Serves 4

¼ cup all-purpose flour
2 teaspoons salt, divided
½ teaspoon ground black pepper, divided
2 large eggs, beaten
2 cups panko bread crumbs
1 teaspoon paprika
½ teaspoon cayenne pepper
8 boneless, skinless chicken tenders (1 pound total)
4 tablespoons unsalted butter
1 cup mild hot sauce
2 tablespoons Worcestershire sauce
1 tablespoon red wine vinegar

1 Preheat air fryer to 370°F.

2 In a small bowl, place flour and mix in 1 teaspoon salt and ¼ teaspoon black pepper. In another small bowl, place eggs. In a third small bowl, place bread crumbs and mix in remaining 1 teaspoon salt, remaining ¼ teaspoon black pepper, paprika, and cayenne pepper.

3 Dredge chicken in flour mixture, turning to coat. Then dip chicken in eggs, shaking to remove any excess. Finally, dip chicken in bread crumb mixture, turning to evenly coat.

4 Spray inside of air fryer with olive oil spray. Arrange chicken inside air fryer and spray top of chicken with olive oil spray. Air fry 18 minutes, flipping halfway through. Chicken is done when it reaches an internal temperature of 165°F.

5 In a small saucepan over medium heat, melt butter and whisk in hot sauce, Worcestershire sauce, and red wine vinegar until combined, about 3 minutes.

6 Remove chicken from air fryer and brush sauce on chicken. Serve.

PER SERVING

CALORIES: 350 | FAT: 13g | SODIUM: 2,682mg | CARBOHYDRATES: 28g | FIBER: 0g | SUGAR: 2g | PROTEIN: 26g

Chicken Kebabs

This simple and delicious chicken recipe combines juicy marinated chicken with fresh vegetables. This wholesome meal cooks quickly in the air fryer, and it leaves less mess to clean up. Plan on letting the chicken marinate for at least 20 minutes and using metal kebab sticks for cooking in your air fryer.

Hands-On Time: 20 minutes
Cook Time: 18 minutes (per batch)

Serves 4

1 tablespoon olive oil
1 tablespoon low-sodium soy sauce
1 tablespoon honey
1 teaspoon salt
1 teaspoon garlic powder
1 teaspoon ground ginger
1 teaspoon chili powder
½ teaspoon ground black pepper
4 boneless, skinless chicken breasts (1 pound total), cut into 1" cubes
1 medium zucchini, sliced ½" thick
1 medium red bell pepper, seeded and cut into 1" cubes
1 medium yellow bell pepper, seeded and cut into 1" cubes
1 small red onion, peeled and cut into 1" cubes

1   In a medium shallow dish, mix together olive oil, soy sauce, honey, salt, garlic powder, ginger, chili powder, and black pepper. Combine chicken and marinade in a zip-top bag and refrigerate 20 minutes or up to 24 hours.

2   Preheat air fryer to 350°F.

3   Remove chicken from marinade and place chicken on skewers, alternating with each type of vegetable. Leave ½" at the end of each skewer.

4   Arrange chicken skewers inside air fryer in an even layer (you may need to work in batches). Air fry 18 minutes, flipping halfway through. Chicken is done when it reaches an internal temperature of 165°F. Remove from air fryer and serve.

PER SERVING

CALORIES: 215 | FAT: 6g | SODIUM: 757mg | CARBOHYDRATES: 14g | FIBER: 2g | SUGAR: 8g | PROTEIN: 27g

Popcorn Chicken

These little bites of chicken are perfectly crispy on the outside with a great combination of savory and tangy flavors. They are marinated in buttermilk before being coated in a crispy-crunchy panko crust that turns golden brown in the air fryer. You can serve this chicken with ketchup or ranch dressing for dipping.

Hands-On Time: 20 minutes
Cook Time: 10 minutes (per batch)

Serves 4

4 boneless, skinless chicken breasts (1 pound total), cut into 1" cubes
1 cup buttermilk
1 cup all-purpose flour
1 teaspoon salt
1 teaspoon paprika
1 teaspoon garlic powder
½ teaspoon ground black pepper
2 large eggs, beaten
2 cups panko bread crumbs

1 In a medium shallow dish, place chicken and top with buttermilk. Refrigerate 20 minutes.

2 Preheat air fryer to 400°F.

3 In a medium shallow bowl, combine flour, salt, paprika, garlic powder, and pepper. In another medium shallow bowl, place eggs. In a third medium shallow bowl, place bread crumbs.

4 Remove chicken from buttermilk mixture. Dredge chicken in flour mixture, turning to coat. Then dip chicken in eggs, shaking to remove any excess. Finally, dip chicken in bread crumbs, turning to evenly coat.

5 Spray inside of air fryer with olive oil spray. Arrange chicken inside air fryer in a single layer and spray top of chicken with olive oil spray. Work in batches if needed, spraying the inside of air fryer and top of chicken each time. Air fry 10 minutes, flipping halfway through. Chicken is done when it reaches an internal temperature of 165°F.

6 Remove from air fryer and serve.

PER SERVING

CALORIES: 279 | FAT: 5g | SODIUM: 276mg | CARBOHYDRATES: 27g | FIBER: 0g | SUGAR: 2g | PROTEIN: 31g

Bacon-Wrapped Barbecue Chicken

This chicken recipe features a nice combination of sweet and salty flavors thanks to the barbecue sauce and the bacon. You will want to make this dish for guests! It will leave them begging for the recipe. For best results, choose your favorite barbecue sauce, as the flavor will stand out in this recipe.

Hands-On Time: 15 minutes
Cook Time: 18 minutes

Serves 4

- 4 tablespoons packed light brown sugar, divided
- 2 teaspoons paprika
- ½ teaspoon salt
- ¼ teaspoon ground black pepper
- ¼ teaspoon onion powder
- 4 boneless, skinless chicken breasts (1 pound total)
- 8 slices bacon
- ½ cup barbecue sauce

1 Preheat air fryer to 360°F.

2 In a small bowl, mix together 2 tablespoons brown sugar, paprika, salt, pepper, and onion powder. Rub mixture over both sides of chicken. Wrap each piece of chicken with 2 slices bacon and secure with toothpicks. Brush both sides of chicken with barbecue sauce and top with remaining 2 tablespoons brown sugar.

3 Spray inside of air fryer with olive oil spray. Arrange chicken inside air fryer in a single layer. Air fry 18 minutes, flipping halfway through. Chicken is done when it reaches an internal temperature of 165°F.

4 Remove chicken from air fryer and take out toothpicks prior to serving.

PER SERVING

CALORIES: 327 | **FAT:** 9g | **SODIUM:** 1,028mg | **CARBOHYDRATES:** 29g | **FIBER:** 1g | **SUGAR:** 25g | **PROTEIN:** 33g

Crispy Parmesan Chicken Tenders

The aroma of these juicy chicken tenders will leave your mouth watering. These crispy tenders can be made ahead of time and reheated in the air fryer at 350°F for 3–5 minutes until warm. They taste great paired with French fries and ranch dressing for dipping.

Hands-On Time: 20 minutes
Cook Time: 18 minutes

Serves 4

1 cup buttermilk
8 boneless, skinless chicken tenders (1 pound total)
¼ cup all-purpose flour
2 teaspoons salt, divided
½ teaspoon ground black pepper, divided
2 large eggs, beaten
2 cups panko bread crumbs
½ cup shredded Parmesan cheese
1 teaspoon garlic powder
1 teaspoon Italian seasoning

1 In a medium shallow dish, pour buttermilk over chicken tenders. Cover and refrigerate 20 minutes.

2 Preheat air fryer to 370°F.

3 In a medium shallow bowl, place flour and mix in 1 teaspoon salt and ¼ teaspoon pepper. In another medium shallow bowl, place eggs. In a third medium shallow bowl, place bread crumbs and mix in Parmesan cheese, remaining 1 teaspoon salt, remaining ¼ teaspoon pepper, garlic powder, and Italian seasoning.

4 Remove chicken from buttermilk. Dredge chicken in flour mixture, turning to coat. Dip chicken in eggs, shaking to remove any excess. Finally, dip chicken in bread crumb mixture, turning to evenly coat.

5 Spray inside of air fryer with olive oil spray. Arrange chicken inside air fryer and spray top of chicken with olive oil spray. Air fry 18 minutes, flipping halfway through. Chicken is done when it reaches an internal temperature of 165°F.

6 Remove from air fryer and serve.

PER SERVING

CALORIES: 281 | FAT: 5g | SODIUM: 1,165mg | CARBOHYDRATES: 28g | FIBER: 0g | SUGAR: 3g | PROTEIN: 29g

Chicken Nuggets

Homemade chicken nuggets are a total comfort food and very easy to make. The melted butter coating the chicken makes this recipe stand out from the rest. It calls for chicken breasts, but boneless, skinless chicken thighs can also be used. To freeze, cook as directed. Let cool and arrange in a single layer on a baking sheet. Freeze for 20 minutes and then transfer nuggets to a freezer-safe container, freezing for up to 3 months.

Hands-On Time: 20 minutes
Cook Time: 7 minutes

Serves 4

½ cup unsalted butter, melted
1 cup panko bread crumbs
2 tablespoons grated Parmesan cheese
1 teaspoon salt
½ teaspoon garlic powder
¼ teaspoon ground black pepper
4 (6-ounce) boneless, skinless chicken breasts, cut into 1" chunks

AIR FRYING FROZEN CHICKEN NUGGETS

To heat homemade or store-bought frozen chicken nuggets, preheat the air fryer to 400°F. Cook 5 minutes, flipping halfway through. Serve them hot out of the air fryer and they taste almost as good as fresh chicken!

1 Preheat air fryer to 360°F.

2 In a medium shallow bowl, pour melted butter. In another medium shallow bowl, mix together bread crumbs, Parmesan cheese, salt, garlic powder, and pepper. Dip each piece of chicken first in butter and then in bread crumb mixture, turning to evenly coat.

3 Spray inside of air fryer with olive oil spray. Arrange chicken nuggets inside air fryer in an even layer, spaced ½" apart. Spray top of chicken with olive oil spray.

4 Air fry 7 minutes. Chicken is done when it reaches an internal temperature of 165°F.

5 Remove from air fryer and serve.

PER SERVING

CALORIES: 395 | FAT: 16g | SODIUM: 742mg | CARBOHYDRATES: 20g | FIBER: 0g | SUGAR: 1g | PROTEIN: 41g

Chicken and Potatoes

This recipe features a starch, a veggie, and meat in one dish! It's a combination of tender chicken, comforting potatoes, and sweet carrots. This recipe can be prepped ahead of time and refrigerated until you are ready to cook it, making it an easy weeknight meal.

Hands-On Time: 20 minutes
Cook Time: 18 minutes

Serves 4

2 russet potatoes, peeled and cut into 1" cubes
1 pound boneless, skinless chicken thighs, cut into 1" cubes
4 large carrots, peeled and cut into 1" pieces
3 tablespoons olive oil
1 teaspoon paprika
½ teaspoon dried thyme
½ teaspoon ground black pepper
½ teaspoon salt
½ teaspoon garlic powder

CHOOSING A POTATO

When shopping for potatoes, look for ones that are firm and smooth without any cuts or blemishes. They should not have any sprouts growing out of them.

1 Preheat air fryer to 380°F.

2 In a large bowl, combine all ingredients and toss to coat.

3 Arrange chicken mixture inside air fryer in an even layer. Air fry 18 minutes, stirring every 6 minutes. Chicken is done when it reaches an internal temperature of 165°F.

4 Remove from air fryer and serve.

PER SERVING

CALORIES: 353 | FAT: 16g | SODIUM: 416mg | CARBOHYDRATES: 26g | FIBER: 4g | SUGAR: 4g | PROTEIN: 24g

Chicken Quesadillas

These Chicken Quesadillas are sure to keep you craving them for weeks to come. With a zesty combination of spices and cheeses, they are a family favorite. The real highlight of this comforting dish is the creamy sauce that's both tangy and spicy. Serve with salsa and sour cream. Good luck eating just one!

Hands-On Time: 20 minutes
Cook Time: 10 minutes (per batch)

Serves 4

- ½ cup mayonnaise
- ½ cup sour cream
- 3 tablespoons pickled jalapeño juice (from jar)
- 3 tablespoons pickled jalapeños, diced
- 2 teaspoons cumin
- 2 teaspoons paprika
- 1 teaspoon garlic powder
- 1 teaspoon onion powder
- ½ teaspoon salt
- ½ teaspoon chili powder
- 4 (10") flour tortillas
- 1 cup shredded cooked chicken
- 1 cup shredded Colby jack cheese
- 1 cup shredded pepper jack cheese

1 Preheat air fryer to 350°F.

2 In a medium bowl, mix together mayonnaise, sour cream, jalapeño juice, pickled jalapeños, cumin, paprika, garlic powder, onion powder, salt, and chili powder.

3 Spread sauce on each tortilla. Divide chicken and cheeses evenly among tortillas, arranging them on only one half of each tortilla. Fold tortillas in half and secure with toothpicks.

4 Spray inside of air fryer with olive oil spray before each batch. Working in batches, place one quesadilla at a time inside air fryer. Spray top of quesadilla with olive oil spray. Air fry 10 minutes, carefully flipping halfway through.

5 Remove from air fryer. Remove toothpicks and serve.

PER SERVING

CALORIES: 744 | FAT: 47g | SODIUM: 1,631mg | CARBOHYDRATES: 42g | FIBER: 3g | SUGAR: 4g | PROTEIN: 32g

Chicken Parmesan

This classic Italian dish is made extra crispy in the air fryer. The chicken is coated in a combination of spices, Parmesan cheese, and bread crumbs and cooked to nostalgic perfection. Then it's slathered in marinara sauce and finally topped with mozzarella cheese that melts perfectly and quickly in the air fryer. Serve this with a side of pasta and a green salad.

Hands-On Time: 20 minutes
Cook Time: 18 minutes

Serves 4

- 1½ teaspoons salt, divided
- ¼ teaspoon ground black pepper
- 4 (6-ounce) boneless, skinless chicken breasts
- 4 tablespoons unsalted butter, melted
- 2 cups panko bread crumbs
- ½ cup grated Parmesan cheese
- 1 tablespoon Italian seasoning
- 1 teaspoon garlic powder
- ½ cup marinara sauce
- 4 (1-ounce, ½"-thick) slices mozzarella cheese

1 Preheat air fryer to 360°F.

2 Sprinkle ½ teaspoon salt and pepper on both sides of chicken. Use a pastry brush to brush melted butter on both sides of chicken.

3 In a medium shallow bowl, mix together bread crumbs, Parmesan, Italian seasoning, garlic powder, and remaining 1 teaspoon salt.

4 Dip chicken in bread crumb mixture so it is coated on both sides.

5 Spray inside of air fryer with olive oil spray. Arrange coated chicken in air fryer, spaced ½" apart. Spray top of chicken with olive oil spray.

6 Air fry 15 minutes, flipping halfway through. Top chicken with marinara sauce and sliced mozzarella. Air fry an additional 3 minutes. Chicken is done when it reaches an internal temperature of 165°F.

7 Remove from air fryer and serve.

PER SERVING

CALORIES: 546 | FAT: 20g | SODIUM: 1,187mg | CARBOHYDRATES: 36g | FIBER: 1g | SUGAR: 4g | PROTEIN: 52g

Southern Fried Chicken

This classic comfort food dish features chicken drumsticks coated in a well-seasoned flour batter and cooked to crispy perfection in the air fryer. Make sure to serve this dish immediately, as it is at its crispiest straight from the air fryer. When cooking, spray additional olive oil spray on the chicken if the flour is still showing through.

Hands-On Time: 20 minutes
Cook Time: 18 minutes (per batch)

Serves 6

6 bone-in chicken drumsticks (1½ pounds total)
4 tablespoons melted salted butter
¾ cup all-purpose flour
¾ cup cornstarch
1½ teaspoons salt
1 teaspoon garlic powder
1 teaspoon onion powder
1 teaspoon Italian seasoning
1 teaspoon paprika
½ teaspoon ground black pepper
2 large eggs, beaten

1 Preheat air fryer to 350°F.

2 Brush chicken with melted butter.

3 In a medium shallow bowl, mix together flour, cornstarch, salt, garlic powder, onion powder, Italian seasoning, paprika, and pepper. In another medium shallow bowl, place eggs.

4 Dredge chicken in flour mixture, turning to coat. Then dip chicken in eggs, shaking to remove any excess. Finally, dip chicken a second time in flour, turning to coat.

5 Spray inside of air fryer with olive oil spray before each batch. Arrange chicken inside air fryer in an even layer, spaced ½" apart (you may need to work in batches). Spray top of chicken with olive oil spray.

6 Air fry 18 minutes, flipping halfway through. Chicken is done when it reaches an internal temperature of 165°F.

7 Remove from air fryer and serve.

PER SERVING

CALORIES: 334 | FAT: 15g | SODIUM: 556mg | CARBOHYDRATES: 19g | FIBER: 1g | SUGAR: 0g | PROTEIN: 25g

Potato Chip–Crusted Chicken

This comfort food chicken dish is juicy on the inside and crispy on the outside. It can be made with plain potato chips or your favorite flavor of chip. Anything goes! For a fun pairing, serve with some Garlic Parmesan Carrot Fries (see Chapter 4).

Hands-On Time: 20 minutes
Cook Time: 18 minutes

Serves 4

1 cup crushed potato chips
2 large eggs, beaten
½ teaspoon salt
½ teaspoon garlic powder
¼ teaspoon onion powder
¼ teaspoon ground black pepper
4 boneless, skinless chicken breasts (1 pound total)

1 Preheat air fryer to 380°F.

2 In a medium shallow bowl, place crushed potato chips.

3 In another medium shallow bowl, place eggs and mix in salt, garlic powder, onion powder, and pepper.

4 Dip chicken in egg mixture, shaking to remove any excess. Then dip in crushed potato chips, turning evenly to coat.

5 Spray inside of air fryer with olive oil spray. Arrange chicken in an even layer inside air fryer, spaced ½" apart. Spray top of chicken with olive oil spray.

6 Air fry 18 minutes, flipping halfway through. Chicken is done when it reaches an internal temperature of 165°F.

7 Remove from air fryer and serve.

PER SERVING

CALORIES: 216 | FAT: 8g | SODIUM: 279mg | CARBOHYDRATES: 8g | FIBER: 0g | SUGAR: 0g | PROTEIN: 27g

Beef and Pork Main Dishes

Beef and pork both taste amazing when air fried, especially with these delicious, comforting recipes. Most of these recipes have you do traditional preparation, as if you were to cook these meats in the oven or on the grill. However, cooking beef and pork in the air fryer makes them crisp on the outside while keeping the center juicy. You don't have to worry about dried-out meat with these recipes! In the mood for something familiar? Try the Rib Eye Steak, Steak Kebabs, or Pepperoni Calzones. If you are looking for something different, try the Cheeseburger-Stuffed Zucchini Boats, Chicken Fried Steak, or Jamaican Jerk Pork. Any of these dishes will be an instant favorite.

Sweet and Sour Pork

Make this traditional Chinese dish at home in your air fryer! This tender dish is served over white rice to complete the meal. Top with green onion for a fresh finish.

Hands-On Time: 25 minutes

Cook Time: 6 minutes (per batch plus 5 minutes to air fry bell pepper and 9 minutes on stove)

Serves 4

- 14 ounces pork loin, cut into 1" cubes
- 5 teaspoons cornstarch, divided
- 1 teaspoon salt
- ½ teaspoon onion powder
- ½ teaspoon garlic powder
- ½ teaspoon dried ginger
- ¼ teaspoon baking soda
- ¼ teaspoon ground black pepper
- 3 tablespoons low-sodium soy sauce, divided
- 1 large red bell pepper, seeded and cut into 1" chunks
- ⅓ cup granulated sugar
- ⅓ cup apple cider vinegar
- 3 tablespoons pineapple juice
- 3 tablespoons ketchup
- ½ teaspoon Worcestershire sauce
- 1 teaspoon oyster sauce
- ½ cup water
- 1 cup pineapple tidbits
- 2 cups white rice, cooked

1 In a medium bowl, toss pork with 2 teaspoons cornstarch, salt, onion powder, garlic powder, ginger, baking soda, and black pepper. Drizzle with 2 tablespoons soy sauce and toss again until evenly coated. Cover bowl and marinate in refrigerator 3 hours.

2 Preheat air fryer to 400°F. Place bell pepper chunks inside air fryer. Air fry 5 minutes or until tender. Remove bell peppers from air fryer and set aside.

3 Remove pork from refrigerator and toss with remaining 3 teaspoons cornstarch. Let sit until cornstarch is absorbed, about 5 minutes. Remove pork from bowl and discard marinade. Spray pork with olive oil spray and arrange inside air fryer in a single layer. Air fry 6 minutes, shaking or turning halfway through. Pork is done when it reaches an internal temperature of 145°F. Work in batches if needed, spraying inside of air fryer with olive oil spray each time.

4 While pork is cooking, prepare sweet and sour sauce. In a medium saucepan over medium-high heat, combine remaining 1 tablespoon soy sauce, sugar, apple cider vinegar, pineapple juice, ketchup, Worcestershire sauce, oyster sauce, and water. Bring to a boil and then reduce heat to medium-low. Simmer 5 minutes, then add pineapple and cooked bell peppers. Let simmer an additional 2 minutes.

5 Remove pork from air fryer; toss in sweet and sour sauce. Serve immediately over white rice.

PER SERVING

CALORIES: 457 | FAT: 11g | SODIUM: 1,092mg | CARBOHYDRATES: 63g | FIBER: 2g | SUGAR: 29g | PROTEIN: 26g

Jamaican Jerk Pork

This tantalizing pork dish consists of a pork shoulder marinated in a homemade Jamaican jerk marinade. It's made with Scotch bonnet peppers: a popular pepper in the Caribbean with a heat level similar to the heat level of the habanero pepper. Beware—this dish is spicy! If you want to experience the Caribbean flavor of this dish with less heat, try substituting the Scotch bonnet peppers with serrano peppers.

Hands-On Time: 15 minutes
Cook Time: 20 minutes

Serves 4

- 4 Scotch bonnet peppers, seeded and roughly chopped
- 1 small red bell pepper, seeded and chopped
- 4 cloves garlic, peeled
- 4 green onions, chopped
- ¾ cup orange juice
- ½ cup apple cider vinegar
- ¼ cup low-sodium soy sauce
- 2 tablespoons olive oil
- 2 tablespoons packed light brown sugar
- 1 tablespoon lime juice
- 1 tablespoon ginger paste
- 1 teaspoon ground nutmeg
- 1 teaspoon allspice
- 1 teaspoon ground cinnamon
- 1 teaspoon dried thyme
- ½ teaspoon salt
- ¼ teaspoon ground black pepper
- 1½ pounds pork shoulder, cut into 4 pieces

1 Combine all ingredients excluding pork shoulder inside a food processor. Process until smooth, about 2 minutes.

2 Place pork in a medium dish and pour marinade over pork. Cover and refrigerate a minimum of 3 hours or up to 24 hours.

3 Preheat air fryer to 390°F.

4 Remove pork from marinade and discard leftover marinade. Arrange in air fryer in a single layer. Air fry 20 minutes. Pork is done when it reaches an internal temperature of 145°F.

5 Remove pork from air fryer, let rest 5 minutes, and serve.

PER SERVING

CALORIES: 296 | FAT: 13g | SODIUM: 279mg | CARBOHYDRATES: 5g | FIBER: 1g | SUGAR: 3g | PROTEIN: 37g

Pork Tenderloin Medallions

Pork Tenderloin Medallions taste wonderful paired with something sweet like Maple Cinnamon Sweet Potatoes (see Chapter 4) or Baked Apples (see Chapter 9).

Hands-On Time: 10 minutes
Cook Time: 8 minutes (per batch)

Serves 4

1 (1-pound) pork tenderloin, cut into 1½"-thick medallions
½ cup olive oil
3 tablespoons low-sodium soy sauce
1 tablespoon minced garlic
1 tablespoon Dijon mustard
½ teaspoon salt
⅛ teaspoon ground black pepper

1 Place pork in a medium shallow bowl.

2 In a small bowl, mix together remaining ingredients. Pour over pork. Cover and refrigerate 30 minutes.

3 Preheat air fryer to 375°F.

4 Arrange pork medallions inside air fryer in a single layer (you may need to work in batches). Air fry 8 minutes, flipping halfway through. Pork is done when it reaches an internal temperature of 145°F.

5 Remove from air fryer and serve.

PER SERVING

CALORIES: 243 | FAT: 16g | SODIUM: 573mg | CARBOHYDRATES: 1g | FIBER: 0g | SUGAR: 0g | PROTEIN: 21g

Steak Bites and Mushrooms

The marinade for this dish ensures the steak stays extra juicy while adding another layer of flavor.

Hands-On Time: 15 minutes
Cook Time: 10 minutes

Serves 4

1 pound New York steak, cut into 1½" cubes
8 ounces baby bella mushrooms, halved
2 tablespoons Worcestershire sauce
2 tablespoons olive oil
1 teaspoon salt
½ teaspoon garlic powder
¼ teaspoon ground black pepper

1 Combine all ingredients in a large shallow rimmed dish. Cover and marinate in the refrigerator 1 hour.

2 Preheat air fryer to 400°F.

3 Arrange steak and mushrooms inside air fryer in an even layer. Air fry 5 minutes. Use a spatula to flip over steak and mushrooms and air fry an additional 5 minutes. Steak reaches medium doneness when it has an internal temperature of 130°F. Remove from air fryer and serve.

PER SERVING

CALORIES: 244 | FAT: 11g | SODIUM: 725mg | CARBOHYDRATES: 4g | FIBER: 0g | SUGAR: 2g | PROTEIN: 29g

Pork Schnitzel

This traditionally deep-fried dish is just as comforting when made in the air fryer. It's breaded in a seasoned bread crumb mixture and air fried until crisp. A light spritz of oil on the outside of the breading helps lock in the moisture, giving you that fried flavor. When shopping for pork chops for this recipe, look for thinner cuts.

Hands-On Time: 20 minutes
Cook Time: 10 minutes (per batch)

Serves 4

4 thin-cut boneless pork chops (16 ounces total)
1 cup all-purpose flour
1 tablespoon garlic powder
2 teaspoons paprika
1½ teaspoons salt, divided
½ teaspoon ground black pepper, divided
2 large eggs, beaten
1 tablespoon Dijon mustard
1 cup panko bread crumbs

1 Preheat air fryer to 360°F.

2 Cover pork with parchment paper and use a meat mallet to beat pork until it is $\frac{1}{8}$" thick.

3 In a medium shallow bowl, mix together flour, garlic powder, paprika, $\frac{3}{4}$ teaspoon salt, and $\frac{1}{4}$ teaspoon pepper. In another medium shallow bowl, mix together eggs and mustard. In a third medium shallow bowl, mix together bread crumbs, remaining $\frac{3}{4}$ teaspoon salt, and remaining $\frac{1}{4}$ teaspoon pepper.

4 Dredge pork in flour mixture, turning to coat. Then dip pork in egg mixture, shaking to remove any excess. Finally, dip pork in bread crumb mixture, turning to evenly coat.

5 Spray inside of air fryer with olive oil spray before each batch. Arrange pork in a single layer inside air fryer (you may need to work in batches). Spray top of pork with olive oil spray.

6 Air fry 10 minutes, flipping halfway through. Pork is done when it reaches an internal temperature of 145°F.

7 Remove from air fryer and serve.

PER SERVING

CALORIES: 357 | FAT: 7g | SODIUM: 644mg | CARBOHYDRATES: 34g | FIBER: 1g | SUGAR: 1g | PROTEIN: 33g

Stuffed Pork Chops

This juicy and flavorful dish is made with boneless pork chops and bread stuffing. It's a simple yet satisfying comfort food dish. You can use either leftover homemade stuffing or boxed stuffing in this recipe. Either option will result in a filling meal. Serve these pork chops with Herbed Red Potatoes (see Chapter 4).

Hands-On Time: 20 minutes
Cook Time: 15 minutes (per batch)

Serves 4

4 (2"-thick) boneless pork chops (1 pound total)
1 teaspoon salt
½ teaspoon ground black pepper
2 cups prepared bread stuffing

1 Preheat air fryer to 400°F.

2 Season pork with salt and pepper. Cut a horizontal slice in each pork chop, cutting about 3/4 of the way through. Fill each chop with stuffing and secure with a toothpick.

3 Spray inside of air fryer with olive oil spray before each batch. Carefully arrange chops inside air fryer, with stuffing facing up (you may need to work in batches). Air fry 15 minutes. Stuffed chops are done when stuffing reaches an internal temperature of 165°F, and pork has an internal temperature of 145°F.

4 Remove from air fryer and serve.

PER SERVING

CALORIES: 338 | FAT: 12g | SODIUM: 1,115mg | CARBOHYDRATES: 23g | FIBER: 3g | SUGAR: 2g | PROTEIN: 28g

Cheeseburger-Stuffed Zucchini Boats

The zucchini in this recipe is basically just a vessel for delicious cheeseburger goodness. The cheeseburger stuffing is made with a combination of well-seasoned ground beef, cream cheese, and gooey melted Cheddar cheese. Serve this with some homemade Barbecue Potato Chips (see Chapter 3).

Hands-On Time: 15 minutes
Cook Time: 24 minutes

Serves 4

1 pound (93% lean) ground beef
½ cup beef broth
¼ cup cream cheese
2 tablespoons ketchup
1 teaspoon yellow mustard
½ teaspoon onion powder
½ teaspoon garlic powder
¼ teaspoon salt
¼ teaspoon ground black pepper
4 large zucchini
1 cup shredded sharp Cheddar cheese

1 In a large skillet over medium-high heat, cook ground beef, stirring occasionally, until browned, about 7 minutes. Drain the fat and mix in beef broth, cream cheese, ketchup, mustard, onion powder, garlic powder, salt, and pepper. Continue mixing until fully combined. Bring to a boil and reduce heat to low. Let simmer 5 minutes or until sauce is thickened and cream cheese is melted.

2 Preheat air fryer to 350°F.

3 Slice zucchini lengthwise and scoop out center. Spoon meat mixture into center of each zucchini and carefully place stuffed zucchini inside air fryer, with stuffing facing up. Sprinkle cheese over each zucchini boat.

4 Air fry 10 minutes or until zucchini is fork-tender and cheese is melted.

5 Remove from air fryer and serve.

PER SERVING

CALORIES: 378 | **FAT:** 20g | **SODIUM:** 669mg | **CARBOHYDRATES:** 12g | **FIBER:** 3g | **SUGAR:** 8g | **PROTEIN:** 34g

Creole Pork Chops

Creole Pork Chops come out crispy on the outside and tender and juicy on the inside. The combination of Parmesan cheese and Creole seasonings adds the perfect zesty flavor to each bite. Serve these at a party, or to the family for a special, comforting meal.

Hands-On Time: 10 minutes
Cook Time: 10 minutes (per batch)

Serves 4

½ cup Parmesan cheese
½ teaspoon salt
½ teaspoon paprika
½ teaspoon onion powder
½ teaspoon garlic powder
¼ teaspoon dried oregano
¼ teaspoon dried basil
⅛ teaspoon dried thyme
⅛ teaspoon cayenne pepper
⅛ teaspoon white pepper
⅛ teaspoon ground black pepper
2 tablespoons olive oil
4 (2"-thick) bone-in pork chops (2 pounds total)

1 Preheat air fryer to 400°F.

2 In a small bowl, mix together all ingredients excluding olive oil and pork chops. Brush olive oil on both sides of pork chops and rub Parmesan spice mixture onto pork chops.

3 Spray inside of air fryer with olive oil spray before each batch. Arrange pork chops inside air fryer in a single layer (you may need to work in batches).

4 Air fry 10 minutes, flipping halfway through. Chops are done when they reach an internal temperature of 145°F.

5 Remove from air fryer and serve.

PER SERVING

CALORIES: 575 | FAT: 24g | SODIUM: 691mg | CARBOHYDRATES: 10g | FIBER: 5g | SUGAR: 1g | PROTEIN: 60g

Herb and Cheese–Stuffed Burgers

These juicy burgers are made with a handful of delicious ingredients. This recipe calls for the burgers to be served on buttered and toasted potato bread buns, but brioche buns would also taste amazing. The burgers may be prepared and refrigerated 24 hours before cooking. However, the buns should not be toasted until you are ready to use them.

Hands-On Time: 15 minutes
Cook Time: 9 minutes

Serves 4

- 1½ pounds (93% lean) ground beef chuck
- 1 large egg
- 1 green onion, thinly sliced
- ¼ cup shredded sharp Cheddar cheese
- 2 tablespoons cream cheese, softened
- 2 tablespoons ketchup
- 1 tablespoon Dijon mustard
- 1 teaspoon salt
- ½ teaspoon dried parsley
- ½ teaspoon dried rosemary
- ¼ teaspoon dried sage
- 4 potato bread buns
- 2 tablespoons salted butter
- 4 leaves romaine lettuce
- 4 (½"-thick) slices beefsteak tomato

1 Preheat air fryer to 370°F.

2 In a medium bowl, mix together ground chuck, egg, green onion, Cheddar cheese, cream cheese, ketchup, mustard, salt, parsley, rosemary, and sage. Divide meat mixture into four equal pieces and shape each into a ½"-thick burger.

3 Spray inside of air fryer with olive oil spray. Arrange burgers inside air fryer, ½" apart. Air fry 8 minutes, flipping halfway through. Burgers are done when they reach an internal temperature of 160°F. Remove burgers from air fryer and set aside.

4 Place buns in air fryer (insides facing up). Air fry 1 minute or until toasted. Remove buns from air fryer and slather inside of buns with butter. Create burgers by placing hamburger patties, lettuce, and tomatoes on buns. Serve.

PER SERVING

CALORIES: 525 | **FAT:** 23g | **SODIUM:** 1,166mg | **CARBOHYDRATES:** 28g | **FIBER:** 2g | **SUGAR:** 8g | **PROTEIN:** 47g

Pizza Burgers

Pizza Burgers are a delicious combination of mini pizzas and yummy air fryer burgers. Children and adults alike will love the delicious combination of two all-time favorite comfort foods merged into one tasty dish. Serve these burgers with some Garlic Mushrooms (see Chapter 4) for a great meal.

Hands-On Time: 15 minutes

Cook Time: 10 minutes (per batch)

Serves 4

1 pound (93% lean) ground beef

4 tablespoons pizza sauce, divided

½ cup pepperoni, chopped

1 teaspoon Italian seasoning

1 large egg

4 (1-ounce) slices mozzarella cheese

4 brioche-style hamburger buns

2 teaspoons salted butter

1 Preheat air fryer to 370°F.

2 In a large bowl, combine ground beef, 2 tablespoons pizza sauce, pepperoni, Italian seasoning, and egg. Mix well and form into four (½") patties.

3 Arrange patties inside air fryer in a single layer, spaced ½" apart (you may need to work in batches).

4 Air fry 7 minutes, flipping halfway through. Top burgers with cheese and air fry 1 minute more until cheese is melted. Remove burgers from air fryer and let rest.

5 Place hamburger buns in air fryer (insides facing up). Air fry 2 minutes or until toasted. Remove from air fryer, slather inside of buns with butter, and top buns with hamburger patties and remaining 2 tablespoons pizza sauce. Serve.

PER SERVING

CALORIES: 577 | FAT: 27g | SODIUM: 953mg | CARBOHYDRATES: 36g | FIBER: 1g | SUGAR: 8g | PROTEIN: 42g

Rib Eye Steak

Rib Eye Steak in the air fryer comes out perfectly tender, and it's simple to make! The addition of the flavorful butter sauce makes it a delicious meal. Serve it with a side of Herbed Red Potatoes (see Chapter 4) and Parmesan Asparagus (see Chapter 4) for a perfect steakhouse dinner at home.

Hands-On Time: 23 minutes
Cook Time: 18 minutes (per batch)

Serves 4

8 tablespoons salted butter
8 tablespoons Worcestershire sauce
4 teaspoons garlic powder
4 teaspoons dried parsley flakes
4 teaspoons black pepper
4 teaspoons salt
4 (9-ounce) rib eye steaks
6 cups sliced white mushrooms

CHOOSING A RIB EYE

When shopping for rib eye steak, look for marbling. Marbling refers to white specks spread throughout the meat. Marbled rib eye steak is the ideal cut of meat to purchase for this recipe.

1 Preheat air fryer to 400°F.

2 Melt butter in a small saucepan over medium heat. Whisk in Worcestershire, garlic powder, parsley flakes, pepper, and salt. Remove from heat. Brush butter mixture on both sides of steaks.

3 Place steaks inside air fryer with mushrooms circled around the steaks (you may need to work in batches). Air fry 10 minutes. Remove mushrooms and set aside. Flip steaks over and air fry an additional 8 minutes.

4 Steak is cooked to "medium" when it reaches an internal temperature of 145°F.

5 Remove steaks from air fryer. Let rest 5 minutes. Serve.

PER SERVING

CALORIES: 672 | **FAT:** 40g | **SODIUM:** 2,964mg | **CARBOHYDRATES:** 14g | **FIBER:** 2g | **SUGAR:** 6g | **PROTEIN:** 59g

Meatball Subs

Make this traditional meatball recipe in an untraditional way! The Italian meatballs are made from scratch and cooked in the air fryer. They come out extra crispy on the outside while staying perfectly juicy on the inside. Adding the meatballs to a hot, filling sub makes them even better. Eat these subs right away for the best taste and texture!

Hands-On Time: 20 minutes
Cook Time: 23 minutes

Serves 6

- 1 pound (93% lean) ground beef
- ¼ cup Italian bread crumbs
- ¼ cup whole milk
- 1 tablespoon Worcestershire sauce
- 1 teaspoon dried basil
- 1½ teaspoons salt, divided
- ½ teaspoon dried parsley
- 1 teaspoon garlic powder, divided
- ½ teaspoon ground black pepper, divided
- 1 (15-ounce) can tomato sauce
- 2 (8-ounce) cans tomato paste
- ¼ cup water
- 1 teaspoon granulated sugar
- ½ teaspoon dried basil
- ½ teaspoon crushed red pepper
- ¼ teaspoon dried oregano
- 6 (6") hoagie rolls
- 6 (1-ounce) slices provolone cheese

1 Preheat air fryer to 350°F.

2 In a large bowl, combine beef, bread crumbs, milk, Worcestershire sauce, basil, 1 teaspoon salt, parsley, ½ teaspoon garlic powder, and ¼ teaspoon black pepper. Mix well and form into 1" balls.

3 Spray inside of air fryer with olive oil spray and arrange meatballs in a single layer. Air fry 10 minutes, turning halfway through. Meatballs will be done when they reach an internal temperature of 160°F.

4 In a large saucepan, combine tomato sauce, tomato paste, water, sugar, basil, crushed red pepper, oregano, remaining ½ teaspoon salt, remaining ½ teaspoon garlic powder, and remaining ¼ teaspoon black pepper. Bring to a boil and then reduce heat to medium-low. Let simmer, stirring occasionally, 10 minutes.

5 Remove meatballs from air fryer and arrange inside hoagie rolls, approximately six meatballs per roll. Top each sub with prepared marinara sauce and 1 slice provolone cheese.

6 Raise temperature of air fryer to 400°F. Carefully place meatball subs inside air fryer and air fry 2 minutes or until cheese is melted.

7 Remove from air fryer and serve immediately.

PER SERVING

CALORIES: 620 | **FAT:** 21g | **SODIUM:** 2,147mg | **CARBOHYDRATES:** 75g | **FIBER:** 7g | **SUGAR:** 22g | **PROTEIN:** 39g

Filet Mignon with Garlic Herb Butter

Never grill a filet mignon again! This recipe for air fryer filet mignon is the only recipe you will need. It makes perfectly juicy and tender steak and is topped with a mouthwateringly good garlic herb butter made using fresh herbs.

Hands-On Time: 15 minutes
Cook Time: 13 minutes

Serves 4

4 (6-ounce, 1½"-thick) filets mignons
½ stick salted butter
1 tablespoon fresh rosemary
1 tablespoon fresh tarragon
½ tablespoon minced garlic
1½ teaspoons salt
½ teaspoon ground black pepper

1 Remove steaks from refrigerator 30 minutes prior to cooking.

2 In a small microwave-safe dish, microwave butter 15 seconds. Mix in rosemary, tarragon, and garlic until fully combined. Use a piece of tin foil to reshape the butter into a stick. Place herb butter in the refrigerator to set.

3 Preheat air fryer to 400°F.

4 Pat steaks dry with paper towels and season with salt and pepper on both sides. Arrange steaks inside air fryer in an even layer, spaced ½" apart (you may need to work in batches).

5 Air fry 12 minutes. Steaks are at medium doneness when they have an internal temperature of 130°F. Remove steaks from air fryer, cover loosely with foil, and let rest 5 minutes before serving.

6 Remove herb butter from refrigerator and cut into four pieces. Top each steak with butter and serve.

PER SERVING

CALORIES: 374 | **FAT:** 21g | **SODIUM:** 1,043mg | **CARBOHYDRATES:** 1g | **FIBER:** 0g | **SUGAR:** 0g | **PROTEIN:** 42g

Steak Fajitas

This recipe is made with flank steak, the best cut of beef for fajitas. It's a lean cut of meat that absorbs a marinade well and gets very tender. The marinade is made of a combination of olive oil and lime juice, along with a delicious combination of seasonings to create the perfect steak fajitas. Serve these with the delicious Mexican Street Corn (see Chapter 4).

Hands-On Time: 20 minutes
Cook Time: 17 minutes

Serves 4

- 2 pounds flank steak, cut into ½"-thick strips
- 3 tablespoons olive oil
- 1 tablespoon lime juice
- 1 tablespoon minced garlic
- 1 teaspoon ground cumin
- ½ teaspoon chili powder
- ½ teaspoon salt
- ¼ teaspoon ground black pepper
- ¼ teaspoon cayenne pepper
- 1 medium red bell pepper, seeded and sliced into thin strips
- 1 medium yellow bell pepper, seeded and sliced into thin strips
- 1 medium yellow onion, peeled and sliced into thin strips
- 8 (6") flour tortillas, warmed
- ½ cup guacamole
- ½ cup salsa
- ½ cup shredded Mexican cheese blend

1 In a medium shallow dish, place steak. In a medium bowl, mix together olive oil, lime juice, garlic, cumin, chili powder, salt, black pepper, and cayenne pepper. Pour marinade over beef. Cover and refrigerate a minimum of 1 hour.

2 Preheat air fryer to 400°F. Arrange sliced bell peppers and onion inside air fryer in a single layer. Air fry 7 minutes, stirring halfway through. Top peppers and onion with marinated flank steak. Air fry an additional 10 minutes.

3 Remove steak and vegetables from air fryer and serve on warmed tortillas, topping them with guacamole, salsa, and cheese.

PER SERVING

CALORIES: 729 | FAT: 31g | SODIUM: 1,022mg | CARBOHYDRATES: 43g | FIBER: 5g | SUGAR: 7g | PROTEIN: 61g

Steak Kebabs

These kebabs are made with tender chunks of sirloin steak that are marinated in a flavorful tangy and sweet marinade. They are then air fried to juicy perfection alongside zucchini, mushrooms, and red onion. Make sure to take the time to soak your wooden skewers prior to cooking, as this prevents them from burning.

Hands-On Time: 20 minutes

Cook Time: 10 minutes (per batch)

Serves 4

2 pounds top sirloin steak, cut into 1" chunks

¼ cup olive oil

¼ cup low-sodium soy sauce

2½ tablespoons Worcestershire sauce

1½ tablespoons lemon juice

1½ tablespoons red wine vinegar

1 tablespoon honey

1 tablespoon minced garlic

2 teaspoons Dijon mustard

8 ounces button mushrooms

1 large zucchini, cut into 1" chunks

1 large red onion, peeled and cut into 1" chunks

½ teaspoon salt

¼ teaspoon ground black pepper

1. Place steak inside a medium shallow rimmed dish. In a medium bowl, whisk together olive oil, soy sauce, Worcestershire sauce, lemon juice, red wine vinegar, honey, minced garlic, and mustard. Pour marinade over steak. Cover and refrigerate 1 hour.

2. Soak eight wooden skewers in water for 30 minutes.

3. Preheat air fryer to 400°F.

4. Remove steak from marinade and thread beef and vegetables onto skewers, equally distributing the ingredients. Place kebabs inside air fryer in a single layer (you may need to work in batches). Sprinkle kebabs with salt and pepper.

5. Air fry 10 minutes. Steak reaches medium doneness when it has an internal temperature of 130°F.

6. Remove from air fryer and serve.

PER SERVING

CALORIES: 645 | **FAT:** 31g | **SODIUM:** 484mg | **CARBOHYDRATES:** 31g | **FIBER:** 3g | **SUGAR:** 15g | **PROTEIN:** 53g

Pepperoni Calzones

This simple yet delicious recipe uses a flaky puff pastry dough that makes these calzones buttery and delicious. It's also easy to customize these calzones by filling them with your favorite pizza toppings. Think: mushrooms; or crumbled sausage, bell peppers, and onions; or ham, pineapple, and bacon. The possibilities are endless!

Hands-On Time: 10 minutes
Cook Time: 12 minutes

Serves 3

1 sheet from 1 (17.3-ounce) package frozen puff pastry, thawed

3 tablespoons pizza sauce

½ cup shredded mozzarella cheese

6 slices pepperoni

HOMEMADE "HOT POCKETS"
These calzones are a tastier version of the frozen version. To make your own, fully cook the calzones. Cool in the refrigerator and then freeze in a freezer-safe bag. Air fry 10 minutes at 375°F.

1 Preheat air fryer to 350°F.

2 Slice puff pastry into three strips along the folds of the pastry. Spread pizza sauce over half of each puff pastry slice. Sprinkle cheese over the sauce and top each sprinkling of cheese with 2 slices pepperoni. Fold puff pastry in half and seal edges using the tines of a fork.

3 Spray inside of air fryer with olive oil spray. Carefully arrange calzones inside air fryer in a single layer, spaced about ½" apart. Spray top of calzones with olive oil spray.

4 Air fry 12 minutes or until calzones are golden brown. Remove from air fryer and serve.

PER SERVING

CALORIES: 532 | FAT: 34g | SODIUM: 426mg | CARBOHYDRATES: 40g | FIBER: 2g | SUGAR: 2g | PROTEIN: 11g

Beef Chimichangas

In the mood for a savory, spicy meal? These Beef Chimichangas are guaranteed to satisfy. Pair them with some tortilla chips and Queso Dip (see Chapter 3) for a filling, delicious meal. They can also be topped with sour cream and cilantro, if desired. The chimichanga filling can be prepared up to 24 hours in advance. Keep the seeds in the jalapeño if you want the dish spicier.

Hands-On Time: 20 minutes
Cook Time: 9 minutes (per batch plus 13 minutes on stove)

Makes 8

- 1 pound (93% lean) ground beef
- ½ medium yellow onion, peeled and diced
- 1½ teaspoons salt, divided
- 1 teaspoon minced garlic
- 1 teaspoon chili powder
- 1 teaspoon cumin
- ½ teaspoon dried oregano
- 1 (15-ounce) can refried beans
- 2 (8-ounce) cans tomato sauce, divided
- 1 (4.5-ounce) can mild diced green chilies
- 1 jalapeño, seeded and minced
- 8 (10") flour tortillas, warmed
- 1½ cups shredded pepper jack cheese

WHAT IS A CHIMICHANGA?
A chimichanga is a popular Tex-Mex dish that is a deep-fried burrito. This take on the dish is essentially the same, only made in an air fryer.

1 In a large skillet over medium-high heat, add ground beef and onion. Cook, stirring often, until beef is browned, about 7 minutes. Mix in 1 teaspoon salt, garlic, chili powder, cumin, and oregano and cook an additional 30 seconds or until fragrant. Drain any grease from the pan. Add refried beans and ½ can tomato sauce. Stir well and remove from heat.

2 Combine remaining 1½ cans tomato sauce, green chilies, jalapeño, and remaining ½ teaspoon salt in a medium saucepan over medium heat. Cook, stirring occasionally, until warmed, about 5 minutes. Reduce heat to low to keep warm.

3 Preheat air fryer to 400°F.

4 Spray inside of air fryer with olive oil spray before each batch. Scoop ⅓ cup meat mixture into center of each tortilla. Roll into a burrito and place seam side down inside air fryer. Arrange chimichangas in a single layer, spaced ½" apart (you may need to work in batches). Spray top of chimichangas with olive oil spray.

5 Air fry 8 minutes, flipping halfway through. Sprinkle chimichangas with cheese and air fry 1 additional minute or until melted.

6 Remove chimichangas from air fryer and top with tomato jalapeño sauce. Serve.

PER SERVING

CALORIES: 461 | FAT: 15g | SODIUM: 1,566mg | CARBOHYDRATES: 53g | FIBER: 6g | SUGAR: 9g | PROTEIN: 26g

Spicy Beef Taquitos

Taquitos come out deliciously when cooked in the air fryer. They are hot and spicy on the inside and perfectly crispy and crunchy on the outside. This recipe includes directions for cooking the beef filling, but leftover taco meat can also be used.

Hands-On Time: 25 minutes
Cook Time: 5 minutes (per batch plus 7 minutes on stove)

Serves 4

1 pound (93% lean) ground beef
1 tablespoon chili powder
1½ teaspoons cumin
1 teaspoon salt
½ teaspoon ground black pepper
½ teaspoon paprika
¼ teaspoon garlic powder
¼ teaspoon onion powder
¼ teaspoon crushed red pepper flakes
¼ teaspoon dried oregano
½ cup medium salsa
½ cup pepper jack cheese
12 (6") corn tortillas
½ cup guacamole
½ cup sour cream

1 Add ground beef to a large skillet over medium-high heat. Cook, stirring often, until beef is browned, about 7 minutes. Drain any grease from the pan. Sprinkle chili powder, cumin, salt, black pepper, paprika, garlic powder, onion powder, red pepper flakes, and oregano over meat. Stir to coat. Mix in salsa. Remove from heat. Pour meat into a large bowl and stir in cheese.

2 Preheat air fryer to 400°F.

3 Place ¼ cup beef mixture inside each tortilla and roll up tightly. Secure tortillas with toothpicks.

4 Spray inside of air fryer with olive oil spray before each batch. Working in batches, arrange taquitos in a single layer inside air fryer. Spray taquitos with olive oil spray.

5 Air fry 5 minutes or until tortillas are crispy and golden brown. Taquitos are done when they reach an internal temperature of 145°F.

6 Remove from air fryer, take out toothpicks, and serve with guacamole and sour cream for dipping.

PER SERVING

CALORIES: 503 | **FAT:** 24g | **SODIUM:** 1,199mg | **CARBOHYDRATES:** 39g | **FIBER:** 8g | **SUGAR:** 4g | **PROTEIN:** 33g

Chicken Fried Steak

This comforting recipe coats steak in a breading reminiscent of fried chicken and tops it all with a creamy country gravy. Serve this with Garlic Toast (see Chapter 3) and Green Beans with Bacon (see Chapter 4) for the perfect comfort food dinner.

Hands-On Time: 15 minutes
Cook Time: 18 minutes

Serves 4

2 large eggs, beaten
1¾ cups whole milk, divided
2 cups plus 2 tablespoons all-purpose flour, divided
2 teaspoons seasoned salt
¾ teaspoon paprika
¾ teaspoon ground black pepper, divided
¼ teaspoon cayenne pepper
4 (¾"-thick) cube steaks (1 pound total)
2 tablespoons salted butter
1 teaspoon salt

CHICKEN FRIED STEAK DEFINED

Although the name may be confusing, Chicken Fried Steak refers to a steak that is breaded like fried chicken and deep-fried, or in this case, air fried. It's delicious and has a richer flavor than chicken.

1　Preheat air fryer to 370°F.

2　In a medium shallow bowl, combine eggs and 1 cup milk. Mix. In a second medium shallow bowl, mix together 2 cups flour, seasoned salt, paprika, ½ teaspoon black pepper, and cayenne pepper.

3　Dip each steak in egg mixture and then in flour mixture, making sure both sides are coated.

4　Spray inside of air fryer with olive oil spray. Arrange steaks inside air fryer in a single layer, spaced ½" apart. Spray top of steaks with olive oil spray.

5　Air fry 14 minutes, flipping halfway through. Remove steaks and let rest 5 minutes.

6　Melt butter in a small saucepan over medium high heat. Slowly whisk in remaining 2 tablespoons flour, remaining ¾ cup milk, salt, and remaining ¼ teaspoon pepper. Cook until thickened, about 3 minutes. Remove from heat and serve over steaks.

PER SERVING

CALORIES: 354 | **FAT:** 13g | **SODIUM:** 1,121mg | **CARBOHYDRATES:** 25g | **FIBER:** 1g | **SUGAR:** 4g | **PROTEIN:** 32g

Marinated Pork Chops

These juicy pork chops take just a few minutes of prep and come out tender and flavorful every time. For best results, marinate the pork chops the night before and let them sit in the marinade in the refrigerator until it's time to cook them. These pork chops can also be frozen in the marinade and defrosted prior to cooking. The chops and marinade freeze well in a zip-top freezer bag with as much air squeezed out of it as possible. They can be frozen for up to 3 months.

Hands-On Time: 10 minutes
Cook Time: 10 minutes

Serves 4

¼ cup low-sodium soy sauce
3 tablespoons packed light brown sugar
2 tablespoons lemon juice
1 tablespoon Worcestershire sauce
1 tablespoon minced garlic
4 (1"-thick) bone-in pork chops

1 In a medium bowl, combine soy sauce, brown sugar, lemon juice, Worcestershire sauce, and minced garlic. Mix until brown sugar is dissolved.

2 Pour marinade over pork chops in a large rimmed shallow dish. Cover and refrigerator at least 1 hour or overnight.

3 Preheat air fryer to 400°F.

4 Arrange pork chops in a single layer inside air fryer so they are not touching. Air fry 10 minutes, flipping halfway through. Chops are done when they reach an internal temperature of 145°F. Remove from air fryer and serve.

PER SERVING

CALORIES: 482 | **FAT:** 13g | **SODIUM:** 629mg | **CARBOHYDRATES:** 14g | **FIBER:** 0g | **SUGAR:** 12g | **PROTEIN:** 56g

Mongolian Beef

This tasty beef recipe brings authentic flavor thanks to the combination of dried chili peppers, ginger, and soy sauce. The recipe calls for flank steak, but skirt steak can also be used to make this delicious meal. This recipe tastes great when paired with steamed rice but can also be served with steamed vegetables or a tossed salad.

Hands-On Time: 15 minutes
Cook Time: 10 minutes

Serves 4

- 1 pound flank steak, cut into ¼"-thick slices
- ¼ cup cornstarch
- 1 teaspoon salt
- ½ teaspoon ground black pepper
- ½ cup low-sodium soy sauce
- 2 tablespoons packed light brown sugar
- 2 tablespoons vegetable oil
- 1 tablespoon minced garlic
- ½ teaspoon ginger paste
- 5 dried red chili peppers
- 2 green onions, thinly sliced

BACKGROUND OF MONGOLIAN BEEF

Mongolian Beef is a popular dish from Taiwan. It is made of sliced beef with a sauce that is not overly spicy. It is typically served topped with green onions.

1   Preheat air fryer to 400°F.

2   Toss steak in cornstarch, salt, and pepper until evenly coated.

3   In a small bowl, whisk together soy sauce, brown sugar, vegetable oil, garlic, and ginger paste.

4   Place steak in a 7" cake pan. Pour sauce over steak and add chili peppers.

5   Place cake pan inside air fryer and air fry 10 minutes, stirring halfway through. Beef is done when it reaches an internal temperature of 145°F. Remove beef from air fryer and serve topped with sliced green onions.

PER SERVING

CALORIES: 309 | FAT: 14g | SODIUM: 633mg | CARBOHYDRATES: 16g | FIBER: 0g | SUGAR: 7g | PROTEIN: 26g

Fish and Seafood Main Dishes

Surprise: You can make some of the most decadent and comforting fish and seafood recipes in your air fryer! You can also re-create your favorite fish and seafood restaurant dishes at home. This chapter has a large variety of dishes to choose from. It teaches you how to make classic seafood dishes like Coconut Shrimp, Crab Cakes, Lobster Mac and Cheese, Crab Legs with Cajun Garlic Butter Sauce, and Mahi Mahi Fish Tacos. You will also learn how to make classic diner food like Fish and Chips and Tuna Melts. Try something new with the Halibut Enchiladas, Chili Lime Tilapia with Avocado Crema, or Mahi Mahi with Lemon Garlic Cream Sauce.

Fish and Chips

Make this traditional pub food recipe in the air fryer. The cod comes out mild and tender with a crunchy coating. The fries (or chips) are air fried until crisp with just the right amount of seasoning. Consider adding tartar sauce for dipping.

Hands-On Time: 20 minutes

Cook Time: Fries: 16 minutes (per batch), Cod: 7 minutes (per batch)

Serves 4

- 4 medium russet potatoes
- 1 cup beer
- 1¾ cups all-purpose flour, divided
- 1 large egg
- 2½ teaspoons salt, divided
- 1 teaspoon baking soda
- ½ teaspoon ground black pepper, divided
- 1 tablespoon paprika
- 1 teaspoon Old Bay Seasoning
- 4 cod steaks (24 ounces total)
- 2 tablespoons olive oil

1   Leaving the skin on, cut potatoes into ¼"-thick strips. Soak cut potatoes in cold water 1 hour, changing the water every 20 minutes.

2   Preheat air fryer to 370°F.

3   In a medium bowl, mix together beer, 1 cup flour, egg, 1 teaspoon salt, baking soda, and ¼ teaspoon pepper. In another medium bowl, whisk together remaining ¾ cup flour, paprika, Old Bay Seasoning, ½ teaspoon salt, and remaining ¼ teaspoon pepper. Dip cod in beer mixture and then in flour mixture, turning to evenly coat.

4   Spray inside of air fryer and both sides of cod with olive oil spray. Arrange cod inside air fryer, spaced ½" apart. Work in batches if needed, spraying inside of air fryer each time. Air fry 7 minutes, flipping halfway through. Cod is done when it reaches an internal temperature of 145°F. Remove cod and cover with foil to keep warm.

5   Rinse potatoes. Pat dry. Increase air fryer temperature to 380°F. Toss potatoes in olive oil and remaining 1 teaspoon salt. Working in batches, arrange potatoes evenly inside air fryer.

6   Air fry 16 minutes or until crispy, shaking or turning halfway through.

7   Remove potatoes from air fryer and serve with cod.

PER SERVING

CALORIES: 550 | FAT: 9g | SODIUM: 1,563mg | CARBOHYDRATES: 71g | FIBER: 6g | SUGAR: 2g | PROTEIN: 41g

Italian Butter Cod

This simple and delicious recipe combines a mild whitefish with garlic butter to make the flavor rich and satisfying. It's an easy dish to make on a busy weeknight that will have you looking forward to your meal and not thinking about how long you'll be in the kitchen. Fresh parsley and lemon make this dish stand out. If needed, 1 teaspoon dried parsley and equal amounts of bottled lemon juice may be used.

Hands-On Time: 10 minutes

Cook Time: 7 minutes (per batch plus 2 minutes on stove)

Serves 4

4 (6-ounce) cod steaks (24 ounces total)

1 teaspoon salt, divided

⅛ teaspoon ground black pepper

4 tablespoons salted butter

1 tablespoon minced garlic

1 tablespoon chopped fresh flat-leaf parsley

2 tablespoons lemon juice

HOW TO TELL WHEN COD IS READY

Cod is fully cooked when it starts to flake apart. Simply poke it with a fork at an angle and twist. It should flake easily and no longer be translucent.

1 Preheat air fryer to 400°F.

2 Season cod with ¾ teaspoon salt and pepper. Spray inside of air fryer with olive oil spray. Arrange cod inside air fryer in a single layer, about ½" apart. Work in batches if needed, spraying inside of air fryer with olive oil spray each time.

3 Air fry 7 minutes, flipping halfway through. Cod is done when it reaches an internal temperature of 140°F.

4 Melt butter in a medium skillet over medium heat. Whisk in garlic and cook until fragrant, about 1 minute. Add parsley, lemon juice, and remaining ¼ teaspoon salt.

5 Remove cod from air fryer and pour garlic butter over cod before serving.

PER SERVING

CALORIES: 245 | FAT: 11g | SODIUM: 765mg | CARBOHYDRATES: 1g | FIBER: 0g | SUGAR: 0g | PROTEIN: 31g

Coconut Curry Salmon

This air fryer salmon is paired with a sweet and savory spice rub and topped with a creamy coconut curry sauce. It's the perfect comfort food salmon recipe. Coconut Curry Salmon tastes great when served over a bed of steamed rice, as it soaks up the extra coconut curry sauce.

Hands-On Time: 15 minutes

Cook Time: 8 minutes (per batch plus 13 minutes on stove)

Serves 4

- 2 tablespoons olive oil, divided
- 2 tablespoons packed light brown sugar, divided
- 1 teaspoon curry powder
- ½ teaspoon onion powder
- ½ teaspoon garlic powder
- ½ teaspoon salt
- ⅛ teaspoon ground black pepper
- 4 (1"-thick, 6-ounce) salmon fillets
- 1 tablespoon minced garlic
- 1 tablespoon minced ginger
- 1 tablespoon lemongrass paste
- 1 tablespoon red curry paste
- 1 (13.5-ounce) can coconut milk
- 2 tablespoons fish sauce
- 1 tablespoon lime juice
- 1 teaspoon lime zest
- 3 cups baby spinach, chopped

1. Preheat air fryer to 400°F.

2. In a small bowl, mix together 1 tablespoon olive oil, 1 tablespoon brown sugar, curry powder, onion powder, garlic powder, salt, and pepper. Brush olive oil mixture over both sides of salmon.

3. Spray inside of air fryer with olive oil spray. Arrange salmon in a single layer inside air fryer, spaced ½" apart. Work in batches if needed, spraying inside of air fryer with olive oil spray each time.

4. Air fry 8 minutes, flipping halfway through. Salmon is done when it reaches an internal temperature of 145°F. Remove salmon from air fryer.

5. Heat remaining 1 tablespoon olive oil in a large skillet over medium heat. Once oil is hot, add garlic, ginger, and lemongrass. Cook 5 minutes, stirring occasionally. Mix in remaining 1 tablespoon brown sugar and curry paste. Cook an additional 3 minutes. Mix in coconut milk, fish sauce, lime juice, and lime zest. Mix in spinach and cook, stirring constantly, 3 minutes, or until spinach is wilted. Serve curry sauce over cooked salmon.

PER SERVING

CALORIES: 391 | FAT: 19g | SODIUM: 1,350mg | CARBOHYDRATES: 15g | FIBER: 1g | SUGAR: 9g | PROTEIN: 35g

Coconut Shrimp

This sweet and crispy shrimp dish is a total crowd-pleaser! The shrimp are coated with a mixture of coconut and bread crumbs before air frying and come out tasting like you're visiting a tropical island. For the best experience, don't skip on the dipping sauce. It really brings out the coconut flavor.

Hands-On Time: 20 minutes
Cook Time: 5 minutes (per batch)

Serves 4

⅓ cup all-purpose flour
½ teaspoon salt
½ teaspoon ground black pepper
2 large eggs, beaten
¾ cup panko bread crumbs
1 cup sweetened shredded coconut
1 pound raw large shrimp, peeled and deveined with tails attached
¼ cup sweet chili sauce
¼ cup apricot preserves

1   Preheat air fryer to 400°F.

2   In a medium shallow bowl, mix together flour, salt, and pepper. In another medium shallow bowl, place eggs. In a third medium shallow bowl, mix together the panko bread crumbs and coconut.

3   Dredge shrimp in flour. Then dip shrimp in eggs, shaking to remove any excess. Finally, dip shrimp in the coconut mixture.

4   Spray inside of air fryer with olive oil spray before each batch. Arrange shrimp inside air fryer in a single layer (you may need to work in batches). Spray top of shrimp with olive oil spray.

5   Air fry 5 minutes, flipping halfway through. Shrimp is done when it reaches an internal temperature of 145°F.

6   Remove shrimp from air fryer.

7   Whisk together chili sauce and apricot preserves. Serve sauce with shrimp for dipping.

PER SERVING

CALORIES: 346 | FAT: 7g | SODIUM: 1,260mg | CARBOHYDRATES: 49g | FIBER: 2g | SUGAR: 24g | PROTEIN: 21g

Honey Garlic Shrimp

Enjoy this plump and juicy shrimp that's coated in a sweet and savory honey garlic sauce. The sauce is incredibly easy to whisk together, and the shrimp cooks in just 5 minutes in the air fryer! This recipe calls for 20 minutes of marinating that allows the shrimp to really soak in the flavor of the marinade. Serve this shrimp with rice and macaroni salad or a side of Parmesan Asparagus (see Chapter 4).

Hands-On Time: 10 minutes
Cook Time: 5 minutes

Serves 4

⅓ cup honey
¼ cup low-sodium soy sauce
1 tablespoon minced garlic
1 teaspoon grated ginger
¼ teaspoon crushed red
    pepper flakes
1 pound raw large shrimp,
    peeled and deveined with
    tails attached
1 green onion, sliced

1 In a small bowl, whisk together honey, soy sauce, garlic, ginger, and red pepper flakes. Pour sauce over shrimp. Cover and marinate in the refrigerator 20 minutes.

2 Preheat air fryer to 400°F.

3 Spray inside of air fryer with olive oil spray. Remove shrimp from marinade and arrange inside air fryer in a single layer.

4 Air fry 5 minutes, flipping halfway through. Shrimp is done when it reaches an internal temperature of 145°F.

5 Remove from air fryer. Serve shrimp topped with sliced green onion.

PER SERVING

CALORIES: 180 | FAT: 1g | SODIUM: 1,042mg | CARBOHYDRATES: 27g | FIBER: 0g | SUGAR: 24g | PROTEIN: 16g

Chipotle Shrimp

This recipe for Chipotle Shrimp brings the heat. This delicious dish is paired with a creamy sour cream dipping sauce that helps curb some of the heat. The shrimp can be refrigerated in the marinade for up to 24 hours before cooking.

Hands-On Time: 20 minutes
Cook Time: 10 minutes

Serves 4

- ⅛ cup packed light brown sugar
- 1 chipotle pepper in adobo sauce, chopped, plus ⅛ cup adobo sauce
- 1½ tablespoons minced garlic, divided
- 1 tablespoon water
- 1 tablespoon lime juice
- 2 teaspoons olive oil
- ½ teaspoon salt, divided
- 1 pound raw large shrimp, peeled and deveined with tails attached
- 1 cup sour cream
- ½ cup minced cilantro
- 1 teaspoon lime zest (from 1 lime)
- ¼ teaspoon fresh minced mint

1 In a small saucepan over medium-high heat, add brown sugar, chipotle pepper, adobo sauce, 1 tablespoon minced garlic, water, lime juice, oil, and ¼ teaspoon salt. Bring to a boil, stirring occasionally. Reduce heat to low and cook 2 minutes. Remove from heat and let cool 10 minutes.

2 Once sauce is cooled, pour over shrimp. Cover and refrigerate 20 minutes.

3 While shrimp is marinating, prepare dipping sauce. In a small bowl, whisk together sour cream, cilantro, remaining ½ tablespoon garlic, lime zest, remaining ¼ teaspoon salt, and mint. Refrigerate until ready to serve.

4 Preheat air fryer to 400°F.

5 Remove shrimp from marinade. Spray inside of air fryer with olive oil spray. Arrange shrimp in a single layer inside air fryer.

6 Air fry 5 minutes, flipping halfway through. Shrimp is done when it reaches an internal temperature of 145°F.

7 Remove from air fryer. Serve with dipping sauce.

PER SERVING

CALORIES: 218 | FAT: 12g | SODIUM: 814mg | CARBOHYDRATES: 7g | FIBER: 0g | SUGAR: 5g | PROTEIN: 16g

Creamy Tuscan Shrimp

This Tuscan-style shrimp dish is made with a great combination of sun-dried tomatoes, herbs, and spices. Paired with a thick, creamy sauce, it's sure to be a favorite for you and your guests! Serve this dish with some Garlic Zucchini (see Chapter 4) for a delicious meal.

Hands-On Time: 10 minutes
Cook Time: 15 minutes

Serves 4

2 tablespoons salted butter
1 teaspoon all-purpose flour
1 tablespoon minced garlic
1 cup heavy cream
½ teaspoon lemon juice
1 teaspoon Italian **seasoning**
¾ teaspoon salt
⅛ teaspoon ground black pepper
¼ cup sun-dried tomatoes, chopped
1 pound raw large shrimp with tails attached, peeled and deveined
1 cup baby spinach
2 tablespoons finely chopped fresh basil

1 In a large skillet over medium-high heat, melt butter. Mix in flour and cook 1 minute, mixing until smooth. Add in garlic and cook until fragrant, about 1 minute. Mix in heavy cream, lemon juice, Italian seasoning, salt, pepper, and sun-dried tomatoes. Let simmer 5 minutes, stirring constantly.

2 Preheat air fryer to 400°F.

3 Place shrimp in a 7" cake pan and pour cream sauce over shrimp.

4 Place cake pan inside air fryer and air fry 5 minutes. Shrimp is done when it reaches an internal temperature of 145°F. Remove from air fryer. Add spinach and basil and air fry an additional 2 minutes or until wilted. Serve.

PER SERVING

CALORIES: 349 | **FAT:** 27g | **SODIUM:** 1,140mg | **CARBOHYDRATES:** 6g | **FIBER:** 1g | **SUGAR:** 3g | **PROTEIN:** 17g

Shrimp Tacos

These light and fresh tacos are packed with flavor! The shrimp cook in just minutes in the air fryer and come out plump and juicy. The tacos are built on charred corn tortillas and topped with crunchy cabbage and a creamy, spicy shrimp taco sauce. Top these with some fresh cilantro and lime juice for a refreshing feast.

Hands-On Time: 15 minutes
Cook Time: 9 minutes

Serves 4

- 1 tablespoon olive oil
- 2 teaspoons packed light brown sugar
- 1 teaspoon salt
- 1 teaspoon chili powder
- 1 teaspoon paprika
- 1 teaspoon onion powder
- 1 teaspoon garlic powder
- 1½ pounds jumbo shrimp, peeled and deveined
- ¼ cup mayonnaise
- ¼ cup sour cream
- 2 teaspoons sriracha sauce
- 1 teaspoon water
- 8 (6") corn tortillas
- 1 cup shredded cabbage
- ½ cup finely chopped radishes
- ¼ cup minced cilantro
- 2 jalapeño peppers, seeded and thinly sliced
- 1 lime, cut into wedges

1 Preheat air fryer to 400°F.

2 In a small bowl, mix together olive oil, brown sugar, salt, chili powder, paprika, onion powder, and garlic powder. Use a pastry brush to coat shrimp with olive oil mixture on both sides.

3 Arrange shrimp inside air fryer, spaced ½" apart.

4 Air fry 5 minutes or until shrimp starts to curl up and hug itself. Shrimp is done when it reaches an internal temperature of 145°F. Remove shrimp from air fryer and cover with foil to keep warm.

5 While shrimp is cooking, prepare shrimp taco sauce by mixing together mayonnaise, sour cream, sriracha, and water in a small bowl. Set aside.

6 When shrimp is done cooking, add tortillas, one at a time, and air fry 30 seconds or until slightly charred.

7 Build tacos by placing shrimp inside tortillas and topping with taco sauce, cabbage, radishes, cilantro, jalapeño, and a squeeze of lime. Serve.

PER SERVING

CALORIES: 401 | FAT: 19g | SODIUM: 1,738mg | CARBOHYDRATES: 30g | FIBER: 4g | SUGAR: 5g | PROTEIN: 27g

Lemon Butter Halibut

Halibut is a mild, slightly sweet whitefish with a firm texture. The air fryer gives the halibut a crunchy crust while leaving the center flaky and tender. The halibut is served with a tangy lemon butter sauce that complements it nicely. Halibut pairs deliciously with rice and Broccoli and Garlic (see Chapter 4).

Hands-On Time: 10 minutes

Cook Time: 7 minutes (per batch plus 2 minutes on stove)

Serves 4

1 tablespoon olive oil
1 teaspoon paprika
1 teaspoon salt
¼ teaspoon ground black pepper
4 (6-ounce, 1"-thick) halibut fillets
½ cup salted butter
1 tablespoon minced garlic
1 tablespoon lemon juice

1 Preheat air fryer to 350°F.

2 In a small bowl, mix together olive oil, paprika, salt, and pepper. Brush olive oil mixture over both sides of halibut.

3 Arrange halibut in a single layer inside air fryer, spaced ½" apart (you may need to work in batches).

4 Air fry 7 minutes, until halibut reaches an internal temperature of 135°F.

5 Melt butter in a skillet over medium heat. Once butter is melted, add in garlic and cook until fragrant, about 1 minute. Stir in lemon juice and remove from heat. Pour sauce over cooked halibut and serve.

PER SERVING

CALORIES: 393 | FAT: 27g | SODIUM: 879mg | CARBOHYDRATES: 1g | FIBER: 0g | SUGAR: 0g | PROTEIN: 32g

Halibut Enchiladas

These creamy enchiladas are filled with mild halibut, green chilies, cilantro, and sour cream. What a delicious combination! Unlike many other seafood recipes in this book, Halibut Enchiladas can be prepared ahead of time. They can be stored in the refrigerator for up to 1 day before cooking or stored in the freezer for 3 months.

Hands-On Time: 15 minutes
Cook Time: 18 minutes

Serves 4

- 1 pound halibut, cut into 1" cubes
- ½ teaspoon salt
- ¼ teaspoon garlic powder
- ⅛ teaspoon ground black pepper
- 1 cup shredded sharp Cheddar cheese, divided
- 2 green onions, thinly sliced
- 1 (4-ounce) can mild diced green chilies
- ¼ cup sour cream
- 2 tablespoons mayonnaise
- 2 tablespoons chopped fresh cilantro
- 4 (10") flour tortillas
- ½ cup heavy cream
- 2 teaspoons all-purpose flour
- ¼ cup salsa

1 Bring a pot of water to a boil over high heat. Add halibut and cook 5 minutes. Remove halibut from water and season with salt, garlic powder, and pepper.

2 In a large bowl, mix together ½ cup cheese, green onions, chilies, sour cream, mayonnaise, and cilantro. Fold in cooked halibut.

3 Preheat air fryer to 375°F. Spray a 7" cake pan with olive oil spray. Fill each tortilla with ½ cup enchilada filling and roll tightly. Place rolled enchiladas inside cake pan. In a small bowl, mix together heavy cream and flour, then pour over enchiladas. Place enchilada pan inside air fryer. Air fry 6 minutes.

4 Top enchiladas with remaining ½ cup cheese and air fry an additional 2 minutes. Remove enchiladas from air fryer. Top with salsa and serve.

PER SERVING

CALORIES: 623 | FAT: 31g | SODIUM: 1,331mg | CARBOHYDRATES: 43g | FIBER: 4g | SUGAR: 6g | PROTEIN: 35g

Honey Garlic Salmon

The salmon flavor is complemented very well with the combination of honey and garlic in this easy seafood dish. The honey garlic sauce is made from scratch and poured over the fish after being air fried for just 8 minutes. Sesame seeds add a nice crunch to the dish. Serve it with some Sweet Potato Mash (see Chapter 4) for a full meal.

Hands-On Time: 10 minutes
Cook Time: 8 minutes (per batch)

Serves 4

4 (1"-thick, 6-ounce) salmon fillets
½ teaspoon salt
¼ teaspoon ground black pepper
½ cup honey
⅛ cup low-sodium soy sauce
2 tablespoons rice vinegar
2 tablespoons minced garlic
1 teaspoon sesame seeds

1 Preheat air fryer to 400°F.

2 Season salmon with salt and pepper. Spray inside of air fryer with olive oil spray before each batch. Arrange salmon inside air fryer in a single layer, spaced ½" apart (you may need to work in batches).

3 Air fry 8 minutes, flipping halfway through. Salmon is done when it reaches an internal temperature of 145°F.

4 In a medium bowl, combine honey, soy sauce, rice vinegar, and garlic. Mix until fully combined. Remove salmon from air fryer. Spoon sauce over salmon and top with sesame seeds. Serve.

PER SERVING

CALORIES: 389 | FAT: 10g | SODIUM: 577mg | CARBOHYDRATES: 38g | FIBER: 0g | SUGAR: 35g | PROTEIN: 35g

Maple Bacon Salmon

Nothing says comfort food quite like bacon. This bacon-wrapped maple salmon is as delicious as it gets. The recipe takes well-seasoned salmon fillets, wraps them in a generous amount of bacon, and coats them in maple syrup. The result is tender salmon coated in a candied bacon that will have everyone coming back for seconds.

Hands-On Time: 20 minutes
Cook Time: 12 minutes (per batch)

Serves 4

4 (1"-thick, 6-ounce) salmon
    fillets
1½ teaspoons salt, divided
½ teaspoon garlic powder
¼ teaspoon ground black
    pepper
12 slices bacon
⅓ cup olive oil
3 tablespoons pure maple
    syrup
2 tablespoons lemon juice
1 tablespoon Dijon mustard

1 Preheat air fryer to 370°F.

2 Season salmon with 1 teaspoon salt, garlic powder, and pepper. Wrap each piece of salmon with 3 slices bacon. Secure bacon with toothpicks.

3 In a medium bowl, mix together olive oil, maple syrup, lemon juice, mustard, and remaining ½ teaspoon salt.

4 Spray inside of air fryer with olive oil spray before each batch. Arrange salmon inside air fryer in a single layer, spaced ½" apart (you may need to work in batches). Brush maple syrup sauce on top of salmon. Reserve remaining sauce.

5 Air fry 8 minutes. Flip salmon over and brush remaining sauce on other side of salmon. Air fry an additional 4 minutes. Salmon is done when it reaches an internal temperature of 145°F. Remove salmon from air fryer. Remove toothpicks and serve.

PER SERVING

CALORIES: 579 | FAT: 36g | SODIUM: 1,529mg | CARBOHYDRATES: 11g | FIBER: 0g | SUGAR: 9g | PROTEIN: 45g

Foil Packet Salmon and Asparagus

Cooking salmon inside a foil packet is wonderful because it keeps the fish juicy. It also keeps the cleanup to a minimum because the foil acts as a barrier between your food and your air fryer. You will love cooking salmon and asparagus together because the flavors complement each other so well, and they both cook in the same amount of time.

Hands-On Time: 10 minutes
Cook Time: 16 minutes

Serves 4

- 1 (¾-pound) bunch asparagus, trimmed and cut into 2" pieces
- 4 (1"-thick, 6-ounce) salmon fillets
- 1 teaspoon salt, divided
- 4 tablespoons low-sodium soy sauce
- 4 tablespoons honey
- 4 teaspoons sesame seeds, divided
- 1 teaspoon garlic powder
- ½ teaspoon ginger powder
- ¼ teaspoon ground white pepper
- ¼ teaspoon red pepper flakes

FOIL PACKS

Foil packs are traditionally a protein source and vegetable steamed together in a piece of foil. This method is often used when cooking on the grill but can also be used in an air fryer. They are easy to prep and delicious!

1. Preheat air fryer to 425°F.

2. Season asparagus and salmon with ½ teaspoon salt. Divide asparagus evenly among four (16"-square) pieces of foil. Top each set of asparagus with 1 salmon fillet. Fold up all four sides of foil so the foil makes a bowl.

3. In a small bowl, whisk together soy sauce, honey, 2 teaspoons sesame seeds, garlic powder, ginger powder, white pepper, red pepper flakes, and remaining ½ teaspoon salt. Pour sauce over each salmon packet and fold foil to close.

4. Place foil packets inside air fryer in a single layer.

5. Air fry 16 minutes. Salmon is done when it reaches an internal temperature of 145°F.

6. Remove salmon and asparagus from foil. Sprinkle salmon with remaining 2 teaspoons sesame seeds and serve.

PER SERVING

CALORIES: 275 | **FAT:** 10g | **SODIUM:** 896mg | **CARBOHYDRATES:** 7g | **FIBER:** 1g | **SUGAR:** 5g | **PROTEIN:** 35g

Crab Cakes

These delicious Crab Cakes are made with fresh lump crab. They make an excellent dinner or appetizer—especially when you're trying to impress guests. If you aren't able to find fresh crab at your grocery store, canned crab may be used. The tartar sauce included with this recipe may be prepared ahead of time and stored in the refrigerator for up to 2 days.

Hands-On Time: 20 minutes
Cook Time: 10 minutes

Serves 4

2 large eggs, beaten
1 cup plus 2½ tablespoons mayonnaise, divided
2½ teaspoons Dijon mustard, divided
1 teaspoon Worcestershire sauce
1 teaspoon Old Bay Seasoning
¾ teaspoon salt, divided
¼ cup finely diced celery
2 tablespoons minced fresh parsley
1 pound lump crabmeat
½ cup panko bread crumbs
1½ tablespoons sweet pickle relish
1 tablespoon lemon juice
⅛ teaspoon ground black pepper

1 In a large bowl, combine eggs, 2½ table-spoons mayonnaise, 1½ teaspoons mustard, Worcestershire sauce, Old Bay Seasoning, ¼ teaspoon salt, celery, and parsley. Mix well. Fold in crab and panko bread crumbs. Form crab cakes into six equal balls and flatten to 1" thick. Cover and refrigerate 1 hour.

2 Preheat air fryer to 370°F.

3 Spray inside of air fryer with olive oil spray. Arrange crab cakes inside air fryer in a sin-gle layer, spaced ½" apart. Spray top of crab cakes with olive oil spray.

4 Air fry 10 minutes, flipping halfway through.

5 In a small bowl, mix together remaining 1 cup mayonnaise, remaining 1 teaspoon mustard, remaining ½ teaspoon salt, relish, lemon juice, and pepper.

6 Remove crab cakes from air fryer and serve with tartar sauce.

PER SERVING

CALORIES: 629 | FAT: 50g | SODIUM: 1,824mg | CARBOHYDRATES: 14g | FIBER: 0g | SUGAR: 3g | PROTEIN: 26g

Lemon Garlic Lobster Tails

Make these elegant and classy lobster tails for dinner tonight. Buttery and zesty, they get a nice kick from the garlic. The trick to making these lobster tails is to use kitchen shears to cut the tops of the tails almost all the way across, but leave the tops attached to the base of the tail.

Hands-On Time: 20 minutes
Cook Time: 8 minutes

Serves 4

½ cup salted butter
2 tablespoons minced garlic
1 tablespoon lemon juice
2 tablespoons minced fresh parsley, divided
4 (6-ounce) lobster tails
½ teaspoon salt
¼ teaspoon ground black pepper

THAWING LOBSTER TAILS

It's best to defrost lobster tails in the refrigerator overnight. They should be on a plate and covered. If the lobster tails need to be defrosted quickly, place them in a zip-top bag in a sink full of cold water. Let sit in cold water until soft.

1 Preheat air fryer to 380°F.

2 Melt butter in a small saucepan over medium heat. Remove from heat and mix in garlic, lemon juice, and 1 tablespoon parsley. Pour half of butter mixture into a small bowl and set aside.

3 Use kitchen shears to cut down the center (lengthwise) of each lobster tail, stopping at the fin. Gently pull the meat up from the shell, leaving it attached to the fin, and place it on top of the cracked shell. Remove any veins or dirt. Season lobster with salt and pepper.

4 Use a pastry brush to coat lobster with the garlic butter from the saucepan.

5 Spray inside of air fryer with olive oil spray. Arrange lobster inside air fryer in a single layer, spaced ½" apart.

6 Air fry 4 minutes. Brush more garlic butter on lobster and air fry an additional 4 minutes. Lobster is done when it reaches an internal temperature of 140°F.

7 Remove lobster tails from air fryer. Serve topped with remaining 1 tablespoon parsley and leftover garlic butter in small bowl for dipping.

PER SERVING

CALORIES: 276 | FAT: 22g | SODIUM: 833mg | CARBOHYDRATES: 2g | FIBER: 0g | SUGAR: 0g | PROTEIN: 15g

Tuna Melts

Tuna Melts taste the best straight from the air fryer, so don't wait too long to take a bite. The tuna salad can be prepared up to 24 hours in advance and kept refrigerated.

Hands-On Time: 20 minutes
Cook Time: 8 minutes (per batch)

Serves 4

⅓ cup mayonnaise
1 green onion, thinly sliced
3 tablespoons minced fresh parsley
2 tablespoons minced fresh tarragon
1 tablespoon lemon zest
2 teaspoons lemon juice
1 teaspoon Dijon mustard
⅛ teaspoon ground black pepper
2 (6-ounce) cans solid white tuna, drained and flaked
4 tablespoons salted butter, softened
8 slices Italian bread
1 cup shredded sharp Cheddar cheese
8 thin slices Roma tomato

INVENTION OF THE TUNA MELT

The tuna melt is rumored to have been invented accidentally in a busy kitchen. The rumor says that a busy cook at a Woolworths in Charleston, South Carolina, accidentally knocked over a bowl of tuna salad into a grilled cheese that was cooking on the griddle. It was served to a customer who loved it, and then later added to the menu.

1 Preheat air fryer to 380°F.

2 In a medium bowl, mix together mayonnaise, green onion, parsley, tarragon, lemon zest, lemon juice, mustard, and pepper. Fold in tuna.

3 Butter one side of each slice of bread. Spread tuna mixture evenly among 4 slices of bread, buttered side down. Top tuna with shredded cheese and two slices Roma tomato. Top each sandwich with a second slice of bread, buttered side up. Secure with toothpick.

4 Spray inside of air fryer with olive oil spray before each batch. Carefully place tuna sandwiches inside air fryer in a single layer, spaced ½" apart (you may need to work in batches). Air fry 8 minutes, flipping halfway through.

5 Remove from air fryer, take out toothpicks, and serve.

PER SERVING

CALORIES: 466 | **FAT:** 30g | **SODIUM:** 800mg | **CARBOHYDRATES:** 23g | **FIBER:** 2g | **SUGAR:** 1g | **PROTEIN:** 23g

Lobster Mac and Cheese

There is no need to wait for your local restaurant to offer lobster mac and cheese on its menu. You can make this comforting casserole in your air fryer in under an hour. The recipe calls for cooked lobster meat: This can be leftover freshly cooked lobster meat or frozen precooked lobster meat. It's combined with cavatappi pasta (corkscrew pasta) and wrapped in a tantalizing cheese sauce made of sharp Cheddar, Gruyère, and Parmesan.

Hands-On Time: 20 minutes
Cook Time: 27 minutes

Serves 4

- 2 tablespoons salted butter
- 2 tablespoons all-purpose flour
- ¼ teaspoon ground mustard
- ¼ teaspoon salt
- ⅛ teaspoon Old Bay Seasoning
- ⅛ teaspoon ground black pepper
- 1½ cups whole milk
- ¼ cup heavy cream
- 1 cup shredded sharp Cheddar cheese
- ⅔ cup shredded Gruyère cheese
- ¼ cup shredded Parmesan cheese
- 8 ounces cavatappi pasta, cooked according to package directions
- 4 ounces lobster meat, cooked and chopped
- ¼ cup Italian bread crumbs
- 1 tablespoon salted butter, melted
- 1 tablespoon grated Parmesan cheese
- ½ teaspoon minced fresh parsley

1 Preheat air fryer to 360°F. Spray a 7" cake pan with olive oil spray.

2 Melt butter in a medium skillet over medium heat. Whisk in flour, mustard, salt, Old Bay Seasoning, and pepper. Cook, stirring constantly, 1 minute. Slowly mix in milk and heavy cream. Continue mixing until fully combined. Bring mixture to a gentle boil and let simmer 2 minutes, mixing constantly. Remove from heat. Mix in Cheddar, Gruyère, and shredded Parmesan cheese and continue to stir until cheeses are fully melted and no longer lumpy, about 1 minute.

3 Add cooked pasta to prepared cake pan. Pour sauce and half of lobster over pasta and stir until evenly coated. Top pasta with remaining lobster.

4 In a small bowl, mix bread crumbs, melted butter, grated Parmesan cheese, and parsley with a fork. Sprinkle mixture over mac and cheese. Cover cake pan with foil.

5 Carefully place prepared pan into air fryer. Air fry 16 minutes. Remove foil and air fry an additional 4 minutes or until topping is golden brown. Remove from air fryer and serve.

PER SERVING

CALORIES: 687 | FAT: 33g | SODIUM: 937mg | CARBOHYDRATES: 58g | FIBER: 3g | SUGAR: 6g | PROTEIN: 32g

Chili Lime Tilapia with Avocado Crema

The combination of chili and lime adds a ton of flavor to tilapia. The avocado dipping sauce adds an extra layer of texture to the dish while cooling down the spice from the chili lime rub used on the fish. This recipe can be prepared up to 24 hours in advance and refrigerated before cooking.

Hands-On Time: 10 minutes
Cook Time: 6 minutes (per batch)

Serves 4

- 2 tablespoons olive oil
- 1 tablespoon plus 2 teaspoons lime juice, divided
- 1 tablespoon chili powder
- 2 teaspoons cumin
- 1 teaspoon paprika
- 1½ teaspoons salt, divided
- 1 teaspoon ground black pepper, divided
- 4 (3-ounce) tilapia fillets (12 ounces total)
- 1 medium avocado, peeled, halved, and pitted
- ¼ cup plain Greek yogurt
- ¼ cup chopped fresh cilantro

1 Preheat air fryer to 350°F.

2 In a small bowl, combine olive oil, 2 teaspoons lime juice, chili powder, cumin, paprika, 1 teaspoon salt, and ½ teaspoon pepper. Mix well. Brush oil mixture over both sides of tilapia fillets.

3 Spray inside of air fryer with olive oil spray before each batch. Arrange tilapia inside air fryer in a single layer, spaced ½" apart (you may need to work in batches).

4 Air fry 6 minutes, flipping halfway through. Tilapia is done when it reaches an internal temperature of 145°F.

5 Place avocado, yogurt, remaining 1 tablespoon lime juice, remaining ½ teaspoon salt, and remaining ½ teaspoon pepper in a blender and blend until smooth, about 2 minutes. Stir in cilantro.

6 Remove tilapia from air fryer and serve with avocado sauce.

PER SERVING

CALORIES: 226 | FAT: 14g | SODIUM: 983mg | CARBOHYDRATES: 6g | FIBER: 4g | SUGAR: 1g | PROTEIN: 20g

Fish Sticks

Fish sticks are a weeknight favorite because they are fast and easy. The fish sticks in this recipe come out fork-tender in the center and are covered with a flavorful bread crumb coating. This recipe calls for tilapia, but any whitefish will do. You can use cod, halibut, or even mahi mahi.

Hands-On Time: 20 minutes
Cook Time: 10 minutes (per batch)

Serves 4

- 4 (3-ounce) tilapia fillets (12 ounces total), sliced into 1" × 2" slices
- ½ teaspoon salt
- ¼ teaspoon ground black pepper
- ¼ cup all-purpose flour
- 1 large egg, beaten
- 2 teaspoons half-and-half
- ⅓ cup plain bread crumbs
- ¼ teaspoon garlic powder
- ¼ teaspoon Italian seasoning

FREEZING HOMEMADE FISH STICKS

Cooked fish sticks can be frozen. Simply cool them in the refrigerator, then transfer them to the freezer, spaced apart on a baking sheet, for 20 minutes. Finally, place them into a freezer-safe bag. To reheat, air fry frozen sticks at 400°F for 12 minutes.

1 Preheat air fryer to 400°F.

2 Season tilapia with salt and pepper.

3 In a medium shallow bowl, place flour. In a second medium shallow bowl, mix together egg and half-and-half. In a third medium shallow bowl, mix together bread crumbs, garlic powder, and Italian seasoning. Dip sliced fish into flour. Then dip fish into egg mixture, shaking to remove any excess. Finally, dip fish in bread crumb mixture, evenly coating both sides.

4 Spray inside of air fryer with olive oil spray before each batch. Arrange fish sticks inside air fryer in a single layer, spaced ½" apart (you may need to work in batches). Spray fish with olive oil spray.

5 Air fry 10 minutes, flipping halfway through. Tilapia is done when it reaches an internal temperature of 145°F.

6 Remove from air fryer and serve.

PER SERVING

CALORIES: 166 | **FAT:** 3g | **SODIUM:** 419mg | **CARBOHYDRATES:** 13g | **FIBER:** 1g | **SUGAR:** 1g | **PROTEIN:** 21g

Crab Legs with Cajun Garlic Butter Sauce

Crab legs are not something you have to visit a restaurant to enjoy. They are quite easy to prepare in your air fryer! The Old Bay Seasoning complements the crab really well, while the Cajun Garlic Butter Sauce gives it that restaurant-style kick you've been craving.

Hands-On Time: 10 minutes
Cook Time: 6 minutes (per batch plus 6 minutes on stove)

Serves 4

8 clusters snow crab legs (4 pounds total)
4 tablespoons olive oil
4 teaspoons Old Bay Seasoning
½ cup unsalted butter
2 tablespoons minced garlic
2 tablespoons Cajun seasoning
1 tablespoon lemon juice
1 tablespoon minced fresh parsley

1   Preheat air fryer to 370°F.

2   Brush crab leg clusters with olive oil and sprinkle with Old Bay Seasoning. Arrange crab legs inside air fryer in a single layer (you may need to work in batches). Air fry 6 minutes. Crab legs are done when they reach an internal temperature of 140°F. Remove from air fryer.

3   Melt butter in a small skillet over medium heat. Once melted, add in garlic, Cajun seasoning, lemon juice, and parsley. Cook, stirring occasionally, about 5 minutes.

4   Remove crab legs from air fryer and serve with butter sauce.

PER SERVING

CALORIES: 430 | **FAT:** 23g | **SODIUM:** 2,491mg | **CARBOHYDRATES:** 2g | **FIBER:** 0g | **SUGAR:** 0g | **PROTEIN:** 44g

Mahi Mahi with Lemon Garlic Cream Sauce

Mild and firm mahi mahi is livened up with a tantalizing spice blend and topped with a creamy sauce. It's a great family dish and may even help convert non–fish fans. Consider pairing it with some Crispy Okra (see Chapter 4).

Hands-On Time: 10 minutes
Cook Time: 10 minutes (per batch plus 10 minutes on stove)

Serves 4

3 tablespoons olive oil, divided
1 teaspoon garlic powder
1 teaspoon onion powder
1 teaspoon paprika
1½ teaspoons salt, divided
¾ teaspoon ground black pepper, divided
4 (6-ounce) mahi mahi fillets
3 tablespoons minced shallot
2 tablespoons minced garlic
1¼ cups chicken broth
½ cup heavy cream
1 tablespoon cornstarch
2 tablespoons lemon juice
1 tablespoon minced fresh parsley
1 tablespoon minced fresh thyme

1. Preheat air fryer to 400°F.

2. In a small bowl, whisk together 2 tablespoons olive oil, garlic powder, onion powder, paprika, 1 teaspoon salt, and ½ teaspoon pepper. Brush olive oil mixture onto both sides of mahi mahi.

3. Spray inside of air fryer with olive oil spray before each batch. Arrange mahi mahi inside air fryer in a single layer, spaced ½" apart (you may need to work in batches).

4. Air fry 10 minutes, flipping halfway through. Mahi mahi is done when it reaches an internal temperature of 145°F.

5. Prepare sauce by heating remaining 1 tablespoon olive oil in a large skillet over medium heat. Add shallot and sauté until soft, about 2 minutes. Mix in garlic and cook 1 more minute or until fragrant. Mix in chicken broth, heavy cream, and cornstarch until smooth. Mix in lemon juice, parsley, thyme, remaining ½ teaspoon salt, and remaining ¼ teaspoon pepper. Let simmer 5 minutes or until thickened.

6. Remove mahi mahi from air fryer and serve with sauce.

WHY IS IT CALLED MAHI MAHI?
"Mahi mahi" is the Hawaiian name for dolphinfish. However, the mahi mahi fish is not related to dolphins. The name "dolphinfish" was confusing for many consumers, which is why it is now more commonly called mahi mahi.

PER SERVING

CALORIES: 375 | FAT: 22g | SODIUM: 1,324mg | CARBOHYDRATES: 8g | FIBER: 1g | SUGAR: 2g | PROTEIN: 34g

Mahi Mahi Fish Tacos

This mild whitefish is brought to life with the creamy and spicy chipotle sauce. The key ingredient is chipotle in adobo sauce—it adds an amazing flavor to the fish tacos. However, a little goes a long way—it is quite spicy! Serve these tacos with some Crispy Chickpeas (see Chapter 3).

Hands-On Time: 25 minutes
Cook Time: 10 minutes

Serves 4

- 4 (6-ounce) mahi mahi fillets
- 6 teaspoons chipotle in adobo sauce, divided
- 4 teaspoons taco seasoning
- 3 teaspoons lime juice, divided
- 2 tablespoons olive oil
- 1 teaspoon salt, divided
- 1 teaspoon ground black pepper, divided
- 1 cup plain Greek yogurt
- 8 small corn tortillas, warmed
- 2 cups prepared coleslaw

1 Place mahi mahi inside a large zip-top bag. In a medium bowl, whisk together 4 teaspoons chipotle in adobo sauce, taco seasoning, 2 teaspoons lime juice, olive oil, ½ teaspoon salt, and ½ teaspoon pepper. Pour sauce in bag, seal, and refrigerate 20 minutes.

2 Preheat air fryer to 400°F.

3 Spray inside of air fryer with olive oil spray. Arrange mahi mahi inside air fryer in a single layer, spaced ½" apart.

4 Air fry 10 minutes, flipping halfway through. Mahi mahi is done when it reaches an internal temperature of 145°F.

5 Prepare chipotle sauce by mixing together Greek yogurt, remaining 2 teaspoons chipotle in adobo sauce, remaining 1 teaspoon lime juice, remaining ½ teaspoon salt, and remaining ½ teaspoon pepper.

6 Remove mahi mahi from air fryer and cut into 2" pieces. Divide fish evenly among warmed tortillas and top with coleslaw and chipotle sauce. Serve.

PER SERVING

CALORIES: 471 | FAT: 18g | SODIUM: 1,192mg | CARBOHYDRATES: 34g | FIBER: 5g | SUGAR: 9g | PROTEIN: 40g

8

Vegetarian Main Dishes

Recipes in this chapter are lacking in meat but not in flavor! There are so many great comfort foods that you can make meatless in your air fryer, including classics like Eggplant Parmesan, Falafel, and White Cheddar Mac and Cheese Casserole. If you want to cook fun vegetarian meals that may be new to your family, try Mexican Zucchini Boats, Avocado Egg Rolls, Chickpea No-Meat Balls, or Spaghetti Squash Lasagna. These recipes are a great way to sneak some greens into a vegetable-hater's meal.

Eggplant Parmesan

Eggplant Parmesan is a wonderful substitution for the more traditional Chicken Parmesan dish. Eggplant has a very mild taste profile and takes on the flavor of all of the delicious ingredients added to it. This dish is best served with pasta and a small side salad.

Hands-On Time: 20 minutes
Cook Time: 16 minutes (per batch)

Serves 4

2 medium eggplants, sliced into ½"-thick rounds
1 tablespoon salt
2 cups all-purpose flour
6 large eggs, beaten
2 tablespoons whole milk
5 cups Italian bread crumbs
1 tablespoon dried oregano
1 tablespoon dried thyme
½ teaspoon ground black pepper
2 cups marinara sauce
1 pound mozzarella cheese, thinly sliced

1   Arrange eggplant slices in a single layer and sprinkle tops with salt. Let sit 1 hour, then rinse eggplant well with cold water and pat dry with paper towels.

2   Preheat air fryer to 370°F.

3   In a medium shallow bowl, place flour. In another medium shallow bowl, mix together eggs and milk. In a third medium shallow bowl, mix together bread crumbs, oregano, thyme, and pepper. Dip each eggplant slice in flour, turning to coat. Then dip eggplant in eggs, shaking to remove any excess. Finally, dip eggplant in bread crumb mixture, turning to evenly coat.

4   Spray inside of air fryer with olive oil spray before each batch. Working in batches, arrange breaded eggplant slices inside air fryer in a single layer. Spray top of eggplant slices with olive oil spray. Air fry 8 minutes. Flip eggplant slices and air fry an additional 6 minutes or until crispy and golden brown.

5   Spoon marinara sauce and mozzarella cheese on top of eggplant. Air fry an additional 2 minutes or until cheese is melted.

6   Remove from air fryer and serve.

PER SERVING

CALORIES: 935 | FAT: 29g | SODIUM: 3,260mg | CARBOHYDRATES: 111g | FIBER: 15g | SUGAR: 24g | PROTEIN: 50g

Mexican Zucchini Boats

Talk about flavorful! These fun zucchini boats are filled with black beans and corn and topped with zesty enchilada sauce. They are cooked until tender and covered with melty cheese. Serve these with some Garlic-Roasted Cherry Tomatoes (see Chapter 3).

Hands-On Time: 15 minutes
Cook Time: 22 minutes

Serves 4

2 medium zucchini
2 tablespoons olive oil
½ medium yellow onion, peeled and diced
1 tablespoon minced garlic
1 (15.5-ounce) can black beans, drained and rinsed
1 (15.25-ounce) can corn, drained
1 cup enchilada sauce
1 teaspoon cumin
½ teaspoon salt
½ cup shredded Mexican cheese blend

1 Preheat air fryer to 360°F.

2 Slice zucchini in half lengthwise. Scoop out flesh of each zucchini half and dice flesh into small pieces. Set aside. Place zucchini halves skin side up and spray with olive oil spray.

3 Heat oil in a large skillet over medium-high heat. Add onion and cook 5 minutes or until soft. Mix in garlic and diced zucchini flesh. Cook, stirring occasionally, 5 more minutes. Remove from heat and mix in black beans, corn, enchilada sauce, cumin, and salt.

4 Arrange zucchini halves inside air fryer (skin side down). Evenly distribute black bean filling among zucchini boats. Sprinkle each zucchini boat with cheese. Air fry 12 minutes or until cheese is melted and golden brown.

5 Remove from air fryer and serve.

PER SERVING

CALORIES: 307 | FAT: 11g | SODIUM: 1,237mg | CARBOHYDRATES: 39g | FIBER: 11g | SUGAR: 9g | PROTEIN: 14g

White Cheddar Mac and Cheese Casserole

White Cheddar macaroni and cheese is made with a combination of white Cheddar cheese and Gruyère cheese. The noodles cook directly in the air fryer in a combination of water and heavy cream. When the casserole first comes out of the oven, it may seem a bit watery. Simply let it sit for a few minutes. The sauce will thicken as it cools. Garnish with parsley for some extra flavor.

Hands-On Time: 15 minutes
Cook Time: 25 minutes

Serves 4

1½ cups elbow macaroni
1 cup water
½ cup heavy cream
1 cup shredded white Cheddar cheese, divided
½ cup Gruyère cheese
1 teaspoon salt
½ teaspoon ground black pepper

PASTA OPTIONS

You can customize this casserole very easily! The recipe calls for the pasta to be precooked, so any cooked pasta will work, including penne, rigatoni, or farfalle.

1 Preheat air fryer to 360°F. Spray the inside of a 7" cake pan with olive oil spray and set aside.

2 In a large bowl, combine macaroni, water, heavy cream, ½ cup white Cheddar cheese, Gruyère cheese, salt, and pepper. Pour macaroni mixture into prepared cake pan.

3 Place cake pan inside air fryer and air fry 22 minutes. Sprinkle remaining ½ cup white Cheddar cheese over casserole and air fry an additional 3 minutes or until noodles are tender and cheese is melted.

4 Remove from air fryer and let cool 10 minutes. Serve.

PER SERVING

CALORIES: 241 | **FAT:** 15g | **SODIUM:** 689mg | **CARBOHYDRATES:** 17g | **FIBER:** 1g | **SUGAR:** 1g | **PROTEIN:** 8g

Avocado Egg Rolls

These meatless egg rolls are filed with a mouthwatering combination of avocado, red onion, tomato, and cilantro. The lime juice brings out all the flavors, and the result is a refreshing egg roll. Good luck eating just one! When selecting avocados, give them a squeeze. They should yield to gentle pressure but not be squishy. If they are rock-hard, they are not ripe.

Hands-On Time: 20 minutes
Cook Time: 12 minutes

Serves 4 (2 egg rolls each)

- 3 large avocados, peeled, pitted, and chopped
- ¼ cup diced red onion
- 1 small Roma tomato, diced
- 3 tablespoons minced fresh cilantro
- 1 teaspoon garlic powder
- 1 tablespoon lime juice
- ¾ teaspoon salt
- ¼ teaspoon ground black pepper
- 8 egg roll wrappers

1 Preheat air fryer to 400°F.

2 In a medium bowl, mash chopped avocado. Mix in onion, tomato, cilantro, garlic powder, lime juice, salt, and pepper.

3 Scoop equal amounts avocado mixture in center of each egg roll wrapper. Dip your finger in water and gently rub the edges of each wrapper. Roll the bottom of each wrapper tightly over the filling. Fold in the sides as you continue to roll the wrapper over the filling. Seal the wrapper by pressing the edges together.

4 Spray inside of air fryer with olive oil spray. Arrange egg rolls inside air fryer in a single layer, then spray top of egg rolls with olive oil spray.

5 Air fry 12 minutes, flipping halfway through.

6 Remove from air fryer and serve.

PER SERVING

CALORIES: 366 | FAT: 15g | SODIUM: 811mg | CARBOHYDRATES: 48g | FIBER: 9g | SUGAR: 1g | PROTEIN: 9g

Broccoli Nuggets

These vegetarian nuggets are a tasty and fun way to get some extra vegetables into your diet. They are made with broccoli, sharp Cheddar cheese, bread crumbs, and lots of seasonings to make them taste their best. Serve these nuggets with honey mustard dressing or your favorite condiment for dipping. Broccoli nuggets can be cooked ahead of time and reheated in the air fryer 1–2 minutes, just until warm.

Hands-On Time: 20 minutes

Cook Time: 15 minutes (per batch)

Serves 4

- 1 (16-ounce) bag frozen broccoli florets, thawed
- 3 large eggs
- 1 cup plain bread crumbs
- 1 cup shredded sharp Cheddar cheese
- 2 teaspoons Italian seasoning
- ½ teaspoon garlic powder
- ½ teaspoon salt
- ⅛ teaspoon ground black pepper

EASY HOMEMADE HONEY MUSTARD

Want a delicious, quick recipe for homemade honey mustard? Combine ⅓ cup Dijon mustard, ¼ cup mayonnaise, ¼ cup honey, 1 tablespoon lemon juice, and ¼ teaspoon cayenne pepper. Mix well and serve.

1 Preheat air fryer to 400°F.

2 Place thawed broccoli in a food processor and pulse until finely chopped, about 1 minute. Add eggs, bread crumbs, cheese, Italian seasoning, garlic powder, salt, and pepper and pulse just until combined.

3 Scoop heaping tablespoons of broccoli batter and roll into balls, then gently press into nuggets.

4 Spray inside of air fryer with olive oil spray before each batch. Arrange nuggets in a single layer inside air fryer, spaced ½" apart (you may need to work in batches). Air fry 15 minutes, flipping halfway through.

5 Remove from air fryer and serve.

PER SERVING

CALORIES: 305 | **FAT:** 13g | **SODIUM:** 750mg | **CARBOHYDRATES:** 26g | **FIBER:** 5g | **SUGAR:** 3g | **PROTEIN:** 18g

Chickpea No-Meat Balls

These "meat" balls have a similar texture to regular meatballs. They can be served as cocktail meatballs on toothpicks or served in a marinara or cream sauce. These meatballs can also be frozen. Simply prepare them to the point of cooking and freeze them instead. Air fry them from frozen, adding an extra 2 minutes to the cooking time.

Hands-On Time: 20 minutes
Cook Time: 14 minutes (per batch)

Serves 4

- 1 (15-ounce) can chickpeas, drained and rinsed
- ½ medium sweet yellow onion, peeled and chopped
- ⅓ cup grated Parmesan cheese
- ¼ cup walnuts
- 1 large egg
- 4 basil leaves, torn
- 1 tablespoon minced garlic
- ¼ teaspoon salt
- ¼ teaspoon ground black pepper
- 1 cup plain bread crumbs, divided

1 Preheat air fryer to 375°F.

2 Place chickpeas, onion, Parmesan cheese, walnuts, egg, basil, garlic, salt, pepper, and ⅓ cup bread crumbs in a food processor. Pulse until chickpeas are diced and mixture stays together when squeezed into a ball, about 1 minute.

3 Place remaining ⅔ cup bread crumbs in a medium bowl. Scoop heaping tablespoons of chickpea mixture and roll into balls, then roll balls in bread crumbs.

4 Spray inside of air fryer with olive oil spray before each batch. Arrange meatballs inside air fryer in a single layer, spaced ½" apart (you may need to work in batches). Spray top of meatballs with olive oil spray.

5 Air fry 14 minutes, turning halfway through.

6 Remove from air fryer and serve.

PER SERVING

CALORIES: 311 | **FAT:** 10g | **SODIUM:** 652mg | **CARBOHYDRATES:** 40g | **FIBER:** 6g | **SUGAR:** 5g | **PROTEIN:** 14g

Vegetable Tofu Skewers

Marinated tofu combined with fresh vegetables makes for a perfectly satisfying meal. The marinade features a combination of delicious spicy and sweet ingredients. These skewers are made with bell pepper, red onion, zucchini, and mushrooms. However, any vegetables can be substituted or added to the skewers. If you're using wooden skewers for this recipe, be sure to soak the skewers in water for at least 10 minutes prior to putting them in the air fryer.

Hands-On Time: 20 minutes
Cook Time: 10 minutes (per batch)

Makes 8

16 ounces firm tofu, drained and pressed
⅓ cup low-sodium soy sauce
2 tablespoons pure maple syrup
2 tablespoons rice vinegar
1 tablespoon minced garlic
1 tablespoon lemon juice
2 teaspoons sesame oil
1 teaspoon freshly grated ginger
1 teaspoon vegetarian Worcestershire sauce
½ teaspoon sriracha
16 baby bella mushrooms
1 medium red onion, peeled and cut into 1½" pieces
1 medium zucchini, cut into 1½" pieces
1 large red bell pepper, seeded and cut into 1½" pieces
1 large yellow bell pepper, seeded and cut into 1½" pieces

1 Cut tofu into 1½" cubes. In a medium bowl, combine soy sauce, maple syrup, rice vinegar, garlic, lemon juice, sesame oil, ginger, Worcestershire sauce, and sriracha. Mix until fully combined. Add tofu to bowl and turn to coat. Cover and refrigerate 20 minutes.

2 Preheat air fryer to 380°F.

3 Build skewers by alternating vegetables and tofu onto skewers. Arrange skewers in a single layer inside air fryer (you may need to work in batches).

4 Air fry 10 minutes, flipping halfway through.

5 Remove from air fryer and serve.

PER SERVING

CALORIES: 105 | FAT: 3g | SODIUM: 305mg | CARBOHYDRATES: 13g | FIBER: 2g | SUGAR: 7g | PROTEIN: 7g

Naan Pizzas

These easy pizzas are made with flavorful naan and topped with a delicious combination of pizza sauce, mushrooms, and baby spinach. They are air fried with a combination of mozzarella and Parmesan cheeses. Serve with the Chickpea No-Meat Balls from earlier in this chapter for a nice pairing.

Hands-On Time: 10 minutes
Cook Time: 5 minutes (per batch plus 2 minutes to air fry naan)

Serves 4

4 (10") pieces naan
¾ cup pizza sauce
½ cup chopped baby spinach
1 cup shredded mozzarella cheese
6 white mushrooms, sliced
4 tablespoons Parmesan cheese
1 teaspoon red pepper flakes

WHAT IS NAAN?

Naan is an oven-baked flatbread that originated in Asia. It's similar to a tortilla, but it is made with yeast and is slightly thicker.

1 Preheat air fryer to 370°F.

2 Place naan inside air fryer and air fry 2 minutes or until slightly crispy.

3 Spread pizza sauce over top of each piece of naan, leaving a ¼" border. Top sauce with baby spinach, followed by mozzarella cheese and then mushrooms. Sprinkle Parmesan cheese over each pizza.

4 Carefully place pizzas inside air fryer (you may need to work in batches). Air fry 5 minutes.

5 Remove from air fryer, sprinkle with red pepper flakes, and serve.

PER SERVING

CALORIES: 380 | FAT: 10g | SODIUM: 823mg | CARBOHYDRATES: 53g | FIBER: 3g | SUGAR: 6g | PROTEIN: 17g

Falafel

This classic vegetarian dish is made quickly and easily in the air fryer. It has hearty chickpeas along with a full-bodied selection of spices, and it comes out tender on the inside with a crispy coating. Falafel can be eaten plain, or it can be made into a sandwich in a pita pocket with tahini, cherry tomatoes, and lettuce. If the mixture is sticky when in the food processor, add 1 additional tablespoon flour and process again 5–10 seconds.

Hands-On Time: 20 minutes
Cook Time: 15 minutes (per batch)

Serves 4

- 1 (15-ounce) can chickpeas, drained and rinsed
- 1 medium red onion, peeled and diced
- 2 tablespoons minced garlic
- 2 tablespoons all-purpose flour
- 2 tablespoons minced fresh parsley
- 1 teaspoon ground coriander
- ¾ teaspoon ground cumin
- ½ teaspoon salt
- ⅛ teaspoon ground black pepper

1 Preheat air fryer to 375°F.

2 Place all ingredients in a food processor and process 20 seconds. Scrape down the sides of the bowl and continue to process until mixture reaches a smooth consistency.

3 Scoop heaping tablespoons of batter and roll into balls. Flatten each ball into a ½"-thick disk.

4 Spray inside of air fryer with olive oil spray before each batch. Arrange falafel inside air fryer, spaced ½" apart (you may need to work in batches). Spray top of falafel with olive oil spray.

5 Air fry 10 minutes. Flip falafel over and air fry an additional 5 minutes.

6 Remove from air fryer and serve.

PER SERVING

CALORIES: 125 | FAT: 1g | SODIUM: 434mg | CARBOHYDRATES: 23g | FIBER: 5g | SUGAR: 4g | PROTEIN: 6g

Buffalo Tofu

This tofu recipe is enhanced with a combination of sweet and tangy flavors thanks to the buffalo sauce. The tofu is air fried to a delicious crispiness and can be paired with rice and the Avocado Egg Rolls from earlier in this chapter. Serve this with ranch dressing or your favorite creamy dipping sauce.

Hands-On Time: 10 minutes
Cook Time: 12 minutes

Serves 4

- 1 pound extra-firm tofu, drained and pressed
- 6 tablespoons cornstarch
- ¼ cup whole milk
- 1 cup panko bread crumbs
- 2 tablespoons olive oil
- 1 tablespoon minced fresh parsley
- ½ teaspoon paprika
- ½ teaspoon salt
- ⅛ teaspoon ground black pepper
- 6 tablespoons hot sauce
- 3 tablespoons salted butter, melted
- 1 teaspoon red wine vinegar
- 1 teaspoon vegetarian Worcestershire sauce

1 Preheat air fryer to 370°F.

2 Cut tofu into 1½" cubes and set aside.

3 Pour cornstarch into a medium shallow bowl. Add milk to a second medium shallow bowl. In a third medium shallow bowl, mix together bread crumbs, olive oil, parsley, paprika, salt, and pepper. Dredge each tofu piece in cornstarch, turning to coat. Then dip tofu in milk, shaking to remove excess. Finally, dip tofu in bread crumb mixture, turning evenly to coat.

4 Spray inside of air fryer with olive oil spray. Arrange tofu inside air fryer, spaced ½" apart. Spray coated tofu with olive oil spray. Air fry 12 minutes.

5 Mix together hot sauce, butter, vinegar, and Worcestershire sauce. Remove tofu from air fryer. Combine tofu and sauce in a large bowl, gently turning to coat. Serve.

PER SERVING

CALORIES: 403 | **FAT:** 22g | **SODIUM:** 1,130mg | **CARBOHYDRATES:** 35g | **FIBER:** 2g | **SUGAR:** 2g | **PROTEIN:** 15g

Barbecue Lentil No-Meat Balls

Lentils take on a similar texture to meat in these meatless meatballs. They are air fried until crispy on the outside and slathered in a sweet and sticky barbecue sauce. Serve these with potato salad and a side of baked beans for a filling and comforting meal.

Hands-On Time: 20 minutes
Cook Time: 12 minutes (per batch plus 5 minutes on stove)

Serves 4

- 1 tablespoon olive oil
- 2 cups chopped white mushrooms
- ½ medium yellow onion, peeled and chopped
- 2 cups cooked lentils
- 1 cup cooked brown rice
- 1 cup plus 1 tablespoon barbecue sauce, divided
- ½ cup bread crumbs
- 1 large egg
- 2 tablespoons fresh minced cilantro
- 2 tablespoons vegetarian Worcestershire sauce
- ½ teaspoon liquid smoke
- ½ teaspoon salt
- ¼ teaspoon garlic powder
- ⅛ teaspoon ground black pepper

1. In a medium skillet over medium-high heat, add olive oil, mushrooms, and onion. Cook until soft and translucent, about 5 minutes. Remove from heat and set aside.

2. Place lentils inside the bowl of a food processor and process 5 seconds or until rough in texture. Add in cooked vegetables, rice, 1 tablespoon barbecue sauce, bread crumbs, egg, cilantro, Worcestershire sauce, liquid smoke, salt, garlic powder, and pepper. Pulse until meatball mixture is combined but still chunky.

3. Preheat air fryer to 350°F.

4. Form ⅛ cup scoops of lentil mixture into balls. Spray inside of air fryer with olive oil spray. Arrange meatballs inside air fryer in a single layer, spaced ½" apart.

5. Work in batches, if needed, spraying inside of air fryer with olive oil spray each time. Air fry 12 minutes. Remove from air fryer and serve topped with remaining 1 cup barbecue sauce.

PER SERVING

CALORIES: 420 | **FAT:** 6g | **SODIUM:** 1,272mg | **CARBOHYDRATES:** 76g | **FIBER:** 11g | **SUGAR:** 30g | **PROTEIN:** 15g

Cheesy Tofu Taquitos

These creamy, cheesy taquitos are just what you need to fulfill your Mexican food craving. They come out super crispy with a flavorful filling made of tofu, cream cheese, lime juice, and salsa. They can be served on their own or paired with beans and rice for a complete meal. They taste great when dipped in guacamole or sour cream (or both!).

Hands-On Time: 20 minutes
Cook Time: 5 minutes (per batch)

Serves 4 (3 per person)

- 1 (16-ounce) package extra-firm tofu
- 4 ounces cream cheese, softened
- 1 cup shredded Mexican cheese blend
- ⅓ cup salsa
- ¼ cup chopped fresh cilantro
- 2 green onions, sliced
- 1 tablespoon lime juice
- 1 tablespoon minced garlic
- 1½ teaspoons chili powder
- 1 teaspoon cumin
- ½ teaspoon salt
- ⅛ teaspoon ground black pepper
- 12 (6") corn tortillas

1 Preheat air fryer to 400°F.

2 Use a box grater to shred tofu into strips. In a large bowl, combine all ingredients excluding tortillas. Mix well.

3 Scoop ¼ cup tofu mixture into the center of each tortilla. Roll up tortilla and secure with a toothpick. Spray inside of air fryer with olive oil spray before each batch. Arrange taquitos inside air fryer, spaced ½" apart (you may need to work in batches). Air fry 5 minutes until crispy.

4 Remove from air fryer. Remove toothpicks and serve.

PER SERVING

CALORIES: 418 | FAT: 24g | SODIUM: 710mg | CARBOHYDRATES: 40g | FIBER: 8g | SUGAR: 4g | PROTEIN: 24g

Spaghetti Squash with Chickpeas and Kale

The spaghetti squash is air fried until slightly crisp and chewy. It's then sautéed with some flavorful vegetables, mixed with toasted pine nuts, and topped with Parmesan cheese. This is a filling and flavorful vegetarian meal that you will enjoy again and again.

Hands-On Time: 10 minutes
Cook Time: 31 minutes

Serves 4

- 2 medium spaghetti squash
- 3 tablespoons olive oil, divided
- 1 teaspoon salt, divided
- 2 medium shallots, peeled and thinly sliced
- 2 cloves garlic, peeled
- 1 tablespoon minced fresh rosemary
- ½ teaspoon red pepper flakes
- ⅛ teaspoon ground black pepper
- 1 (15.5-ounce) can chickpeas, drained and rinsed
- 4 cups chopped kale
- 2 tablespoons lemon juice
- ½ cup chopped sun-dried tomatoes
- ½ cup toasted pine nuts
- ½ cup grated Parmesan cheese

CHOOSING A RIPE SPAGHETTI SQUASH

When shopping for spaghetti squash, look for one that is dark yellow and feels heavy when lifted up. It should not have any cracks or blemishes on the skin.

1 Preheat air fryer to 360°F.

2 Cut thin slices off each end of spaghetti squash and then cut in half lengthwise. Place squash inside air fryer, cut side up. Drizzle squash with 1 tablespoon olive oil and ½ teaspoon salt. Air fry 20 minutes or until fork-tender. Remove from air fryer.

3 Heat remaining 2 tablespoons olive oil in a large skillet over medium heat. Add shallots, garlic cloves, rosemary, red pepper flakes, remaining ½ teaspoon salt, and black pepper. Cook until shallot is soft, about 4 minutes. Mix in chickpeas and cook until golden brown, about 3 minutes. Remove the garlic cloves. Mix in the kale and lemon juice and stir. Cook until the kale starts to wilt, about 3 minutes.

4 Scoop out strands of spaghetti squash using a fork and add to skillet. Mix in sun-dried tomatoes and pine nuts. Serve topped with grated Parmesan cheese.

PER SERVING

CALORIES: 455 | FAT: 24g | SODIUM: 1,020mg | CARBOHYDRATES: 45g | FIBER: 10g | SUGAR: 14g | PROTEIN: 14g

Black Bean and Sweet Potato Taquitos

You'll keep coming back to these delicious Black Bean and Sweet Potato Taquitos. Serve them with Garlic Mushrooms (see Chapter 4) for a full, delicious meal.

Hands-On Time: 25 minutes

Cook Time: 5 minutes (per batch plus 15 minutes to air fry sweet potatoes and 14 minutes on stove)

Makes 16

3 medium sweet potatoes, peeled and diced

2 tablespoons olive oil, divided

1¼ teaspoons salt, divided

½ teaspoon chili powder

1 tablespoon minced garlic

1 (15-ounce) can black beans, not drained

1 teaspoon cumin

½ teaspoon oregano

16 (6") corn tortillas

2 medium avocados, peeled, halved, and pitted

½ cup sour cream

1 tablespoon lime juice

1. Preheat air fryer to 400°F.

2. In a large bowl, toss sweet potatoes in 1 tablespoon olive oil, ½ teaspoon salt, and chili powder. Arrange sweet potatoes inside air fryer and air fry 15 minutes, shaking or turning every 5 minutes. Remove from air fryer and set aside.

3. Heat remaining 1 tablespoon olive oil in a medium skillet over medium-high heat. Add minced garlic and cook until fragrant, about 1 minute. Mix in black beans with liquid, ½ teaspoon salt, cumin, and oregano. Bring mixture to a boil and reduce heat to a simmer. Let simmer 10 minutes. Remove from heat and mix in cooked sweet potatoes.

4. Scoop ¼ cup black bean mixture into the center of each tortilla. Roll up tortilla and secure with a toothpick. Spray inside of air fryer with olive oil spray before each batch. Arrange taquitos inside air fryer, spaced ½" apart (you may need to work in batches).

5. Air fry 5 minutes or until crispy. Remove from air fryer.

6. To make sauce, place avocados, sour cream, lime juice, and remaining ¼ teaspoon salt in bowl of food processor. Process until smooth.

7. Remove toothpicks from taquitos and serve drizzled with avocado sauce.

PER SERVING

CALORIES: 154 | FAT: 6g | SODIUM: 309mg | CARBOHYDRATES: 22g | FIBER: 5g | SUGAR: 2g | PROTEIN: 4g

Tater Tot Casserole

This classic Midwestern dish is known as a Tater Tot Casserole or "hot dish." This casserole is also very versatile. Additional sautéed vegetables can be added, if desired.

Hands-On Time: 15 minutes
Cook Time: 18 minutes

Serves 4

2 tablespoons olive oil
1 large yellow onion, peeled and chopped
3 large stalks celery, chopped
1 teaspoon paprika
½ teaspoon salt
½ teaspoon ground black pepper
1 (20-ounce) can cream of mushroom soup
1 (28-ounce) bag Tater Tots
1 cup shredded sharp Cheddar cheese

1 Preheat air fryer to 400°F.

2 Heat oil in a large skillet over medium-high heat. Add onion and celery to skillet. Cook, stirring occasionally, until onion is soft and translucent, about 5 minutes. Season vegetables with paprika, salt, and pepper. Mix in cream of mushroom soup and remove from heat.

3 Arrange Tater Tots in a single layer inside a 7" cake pan. Place cake pan inside air fryer. Air fry 7 minutes.

4 Top Tater Tots with vegetable mixture and air fry an additional 3 minutes. Sprinkle cheese over casserole and air fry 3 more minutes or until cheese is melted.

5 Remove from air fryer and let cool 5 minutes. Serve.

PER SERVING

CALORIES: 607 | FAT: 41g | SODIUM: 2,469mg | CARBOHYDRATES: 45g | FIBER: 7g | SUGAR: 5g | PROTEIN: 12g

Mediterranean Frittata

Feeling breakfast for dinner? This frittata is made with a delicious combination of fresh vegetables, including zucchini, red pepper, and broccoli. They are air fried until tender and then cooked inside the frittata to make a cheesy and hearty meal. This recipe is very versatile and can be used with any vegetables you have on hand. Serve alongside Sweet Potato Mash (see Chapter 4) for a delicious meal.

Hands-On Time: 15 minutes
Cook Time: 25 minutes

Serves 4

1 small red bell pepper,
  seeded and chopped
1 small zucchini, diced
1 green onion, sliced
1 cup broccoli florets
1 tablespoon olive oil
¾ teaspoon salt, divided
4 large eggs
¼ cup crumbled feta cheese
½ teaspoon dried parsley
⅛ teaspoon dried thyme
⅛ teaspoon ground black
  pepper

1 Preheat air fryer to 360°F. Spray a 7" cake pan with olive oil spray and set aside.

2 Combine bell pepper, zucchini, green onion, broccoli, olive oil, and ¼ teaspoon salt in a medium bowl. Mix until evenly coated with oil. Pour vegetables into air fryer and air fry 5 minutes. Remove from air fryer and set aside.

3 In a large bowl, mix together eggs, feta, parsley, thyme, pepper, and remaining ½ teaspoon salt. Pour egg mixture into cake pan. Place cake pan inside air fryer and air fry 2 minutes.

4 Remove cake pan from air fryer. Pour cooked vegetables into egg mixture and air fry an additional 18 minutes. Let rest 5 minutes and serve.

PER SERVING

CALORIES: 145 | FAT: 10g | SODIUM: 604mg | CARBOHYDRATES: 5g | FIBER: 1g | SUGAR: 3g | PROTEIN: 9g

Vegetable Potpie

Make this delicious Vegetable Potpie for dinner tonight! It's made with a creamy sauce filled with a tasty combination of diced potatoes and mixed vegetables that is topped with a flaky biscuit topping. This homemade potpie tastes great as leftovers too!

Hands-On Time: 20 minutes
Cook Time: 10 minutes

Serves 4

- 1 (6-ounce) package refrigerated biscuit dough
- 1 large russet potato, peeled and diced
- 1 (10-ounce) bag frozen mixed vegetables
- 1 (10½ ounce) can cream of mushroom soup
- ½ teaspoon salt
- ¼ teaspoon ground black pepper

1 Preheat air fryer to 425°F. Spray a 7" cake pan with olive oil spray and set aside.

2 Open the biscuit dough package and separate the dough into two equal portions. Use a rolling pin to roll out each portion of dough into a 7" round. Press one of the rounds of biscuit dough into the bottom of prepared cake pan. Air fry 3 minutes.

3 Reduce the air fryer temperature to 330°F.

4 In a large bowl, combine potato, vegetables, soup, salt, and pepper and mix. Pour potpie filling into cake pan. Top potpie filling with the second round of biscuit dough.

5 Place potpie in air fryer and air fry 7 minutes or until topping is golden brown and filling is hot and bubbly.

6 Remove from air fryer and let rest 10 minutes. Serve.

PER SERVING

CALORIES: 276 | FAT: 8g | SODIUM: 1,254mg | CARBOHYDRATES: 43g | FIBER: 4g | SUGAR: 4g | PROTEIN: 7g

Thai-Style Tofu with Peanut Sauce

The best way to cook tofu is in the air fryer. Air fryer tofu comes out crispier than it would by baking or panfrying it, and it cooks quickly. This Thai-inspired recipe combines crispy tofu with a homemade peanut sauce that's both creamy and spicy. Pair it with some rice noodles for a full meal.

Hands-On Time: 10 minutes
Cook Time: 12 minutes

Serves 4

- 1 pound extra-firm tofu, drained and pressed
- 5 tablespoons low-sodium soy sauce, divided
- 3 tablespoons rice vinegar
- 1 tablespoon pure maple syrup
- 1½ teaspoons cornstarch
- ½ teaspoon curry powder
- ½ teaspoon paprika
- ½ teaspoon salt
- ¼ teaspoon ground black pepper
- 3 tablespoons creamy peanut butter
- 1 teaspoon sesame oil
- 3 tablespoons hot water
- 1 teaspoon minced garlic
- 1 teaspoon ginger paste
- ½ teaspoon crushed red pepper
- 1 teaspoon sesame seeds

1 Cut tofu into 1" cubes and place cubes in a large bowl. In a medium bowl, whisk together 4 tablespoons soy sauce, rice vinegar, and maple syrup. Pour sauce over tofu and turn to coat. Refrigerate marinated tofu 20 minutes.

2 In a small bowl, combine cornstarch, curry powder, paprika, salt, and pepper. Mix well.

3 Preheat air fryer to 380°F.

4 Drain marinade from tofu. Dip each piece of tofu into cornstarch mixture, coating evenly. Set aside.

5 Spray inside of air fryer with olive oil spray. Arrange tofu inside air fryer in an even layer, spaced ½" apart. Air fry 12 minutes, flipping halfway through.

6 In a small bowl, whisk together peanut butter, sesame oil, remaining 1 tablespoon soy sauce, and hot water. Add in garlic, ginger, and crushed red pepper. Mix well.

7 Remove tofu from air fryer. Pour peanut sauce over tofu and top with sesame seeds. Serve.

PER SERVING

CALORIES: 209 | **FAT:** 13g | **SODIUM:** 454mg | **CARBOHYDRATES:** 9g | **FIBER:** 2g | **SUGAR:** 3g | **PROTEIN:** 15g

Teriyaki Rice Bowls

Enjoy this restaurant-style favorite at home! These teriyaki bowls are made with tender vegetables and a flavorful sauce. They're served over brown rice for the ultimate comforting and easy vegetarian dinner. If you want to add more protein to this dish, try adding some cooked tofu to your teriyaki bowls!

Hands-On Time: 15 minutes
Cook Time: 12 minutes

Serves 4

- 1 medium head broccoli, cut into small florets
- ½ pound green beans, trimmed
- 1 large carrot, peeled and sliced
- 1 tablespoon olive oil
- ½ teaspoon salt
- ½ cup low-sodium soy sauce
- ½ cup rice vinegar
- ½ cup packed light brown sugar
- 1 tablespoon cornstarch
- 1 teaspoon sesame seeds
- 1 teaspoon minced garlic
- ¼ teaspoon garlic powder
- 2 cups cooked brown rice

1 Preheat air fryer to 370°F.

2 Toss broccoli, green beans, and carrot in oil and salt in a large bowl. Place vegetables inside air fryer and air fry 12 minutes, shaking or turning halfway through. Remove from air fryer.

3 In a small bowl, mix together soy sauce, rice vinegar, brown sugar, cornstarch, sesame seeds, minced garlic, and garlic powder. Pour sauce over air fryer vegetables. Serve over brown rice.

PER SERVING

CALORIES: 354 | **FAT:** 5g | **SODIUM:** 2,116mg | **CARBOHYDRATES:** 69g | **FIBER:** 8g | **SUGAR:** 32g | **PROTEIN:** 10g

Apple Cheddar Frittata

This quick and easy frittata is anything but boring. The combination of sweet apples and white Cheddar cheese makes this frittata taste elegant enough for a fancy breakfast. You can also make this dish as an excellent dinner that's both filling and tasty. If you can't get your hands on white Cheddar cheese, then sharp Cheddar may be substituted.

Hands-On Time: 10 minutes
Cook Time: 20 minutes

Serves 4

4 large eggs
½ cup shredded white Cheddar cheese, divided
¾ teaspoon salt
¼ teaspoon ground black pepper
1 Gala apple, peeled, cored, and diced

1   Preheat air fryer to 360°F. Spray a 7" cake pan with olive oil spray and set aside.

2   Mix together eggs, ¼ cup cheese, salt, and pepper in a large bowl. Pour mixture into prepared cake pan.

3   Place pan inside air fryer and air fry 2 minutes.

4   Remove pan from air fryer. Arrange apples in cake pan in a single layer and top with remaining ¼ cup cheese. Air fry an additional 18 minutes.

5   Remove pan from air fryer, let rest 5 minutes, and serve.

PER SERVING

CALORIES: 148 | FAT: 8g | SODIUM: 597mg | CARBOHYDRATES: 6g | FIBER: 1g | SUGAR: 4g | PROTEIN: 10g

Soy Crumble Teriyaki Zucchini Boats

These mouthwatering zucchini boats are made with tofu soy crumbles, fresh vegetables, and a delicious sauce made of soy sauce, apple cider vinegar, and agave nectar. They taste best fresh from the air fryer, but the zucchini can be sliced and cored ahead of time and stored in the refrigerator for up to 2 days.

Hands-On Time: 15 minutes
Cook Time: 18 minutes

Serves 4

2 large zucchini
1 tablespoon olive oil
½ medium red bell pepper, seeded and diced
1 green onion, sliced
½ cup water chestnuts, diced
2 tablespoons low-sodium soy sauce
½ tablespoon apple cider vinegar
½ tablespoon agave nectar
¼ teaspoon ginger
½ cup soy crumbles
1 tablespoon sesame seeds

SOY CRUMBLES

These crumbles resemble cooked ground meat and can be found in the frozen section of your grocery store. They are sometimes labeled as "meatless" or "beefless" ground crumbles. They are a great alternative to ground beef.

1 Preheat air fryer to 360°F.

2 Slice zucchini in half lengthwise. Scoop out flesh of each zucchini half. Dice flesh into small pieces and set aside. Place zucchini halves skin side up and spray with olive oil spray. Place zucchini, cut side up, in air fryer and air fry 10 minutes.

3 Heat oil in a large skillet over medium-high heat. Add bell pepper, green onion, water chestnuts, soy sauce, apple cider vinegar, agave nectar, and ginger to oil. Cook, stirring occasionally, 5 minutes. Remove from heat. Mix in soy crumbles.

4 Fill zucchini boats with vegetable soy mixture. Carefully place filled zucchini boats inside air fryer and air fry 2 minutes. Remove from air fryer, top with sesame seeds, and serve.

PER SERVING

CALORIES: 115 | FAT: 5g | SODIUM: 290mg | CARBOHYDRATES: 12g | FIBER: 3g | SUGAR: 7g | PROTEIN: 6g

Southwest Vegetable Quesadillas

These quesadillas are loaded with tender bell pepper, black beans, corn, and onions and seasoned to perfection. The tortillas come out of the air fryer crispy, and the cheese is melted deliciously. Serve with salsa, guacamole, and sour cream.

Hands-On Time: 10 minutes

Cook Time: 10 minutes (per batch plus 5 minutes on stove)

Serves 4

- 1 tablespoon olive oil
- 1 medium red bell pepper, seeded and diced
- ½ (15-ounce) can black beans, drained and rinsed
- ½ cup corn
- ½ cup diced yellow onion
- 1 tablespoon minced garlic
- 1 teaspoon cumin
- 1 teaspoon chili powder
- ½ teaspoon salt
- ⅛ teaspoon ground black pepper
- 1 cup shredded Colby jack cheese
- 1 cup shredded pepper jack cheese
- 4 (10") flour tortillas

1 Preheat air fryer to 350°F.

2 Heat olive oil in a large skillet over medium-high heat. Add bell pepper, black beans, corn, onion, garlic, cumin, chili powder, salt, and black pepper. Cook, stirring occasionally, 5 minutes or until bell pepper is soft and onion is translucent.

3 Divide vegetables and cheeses evenly among tortillas, placing them on only one half of the tortilla. Fold tortillas in half and secure with toothpicks.

4 Spray inside of air fryer with olive oil spray before each batch. Working in batches, place one quesadilla at a time inside air fryer. Spray top of quesadilla with olive oil spray.

5 Air fry 10 minutes, carefully flipping halfway through.

6 Remove from air fryer, remove toothpicks, and serve.

PER SERVING

CALORIES: 543 | **FAT:** 25g | **SODIUM:** 1,319mg | **CARBOHYDRATES:** 54g | **FIBER:** 7g | **SUGAR:** 5g | **PROTEIN:** 24g

Spaghetti Squash Lasagna

Enjoy this vegetarian-style lasagna cooked inside of a spaghetti squash. The lasagna is made with layers of mushrooms and marinara sauce and uses the spaghetti squash strands in place of lasagna noodles. Serve it with a salad for a complete meal.

Hands-On Time: 15 minutes
Cook Time: 40 minutes

Serves 4

- 2 medium spaghetti squash
- 3 tablespoons olive oil, divided
- 1 teaspoon salt, divided
- 1 large yellow onion, peeled and chopped
- 2 tablespoons minced garlic
- 1 pound white mushrooms, sliced
- 1 (32-ounce) jar marinara sauce
- ½ cup grated Parmesan cheese
- 2 cups grated mozzarella cheese
- 1 cup ricotta cheese

1   Preheat air fryer to 360°F.

2   Cut thin slices off each end of spaghetti squash and then cut in half lengthwise. Place squash inside air fryer, cut side up. Drizzle squash with 1 tablespoon olive oil and ½ teaspoon salt. Air fry 20 minutes or until fork-tender.

3   In a large skillet over medium heat, heat remaining 2 tablespoons olive oil. Add onion and cook 3 minutes, stirring occasionally, or until soft. Mix in garlic and cook an additional 1 minute. Mix in mushrooms and cook until soft, about 5 minutes. Stir in marinara sauce and cook until warmed through, about 5 minutes.

4   Scoop out strands of spaghetti squash using a fork and add to a large bowl. Mix in grated Parmesan cheese and remaining ½ teaspoon salt. Scoop 1/8 of spaghetti squash mixture into squash shells and top with 1/8 of the marinara mixture. Top with ¼ cup mozzarella and ¼ cup ricotta. Repeat with remaining squash, marinara, mozzarella, and ricotta.

5   Carefully place spaghetti squash lasagnas inside air fryer (you may need to work in batches). Air fry 6 minutes or until cheese is golden brown. Serve.

PER SERVING

CALORIES: 639 | FAT: 32g | SODIUM: 2,321mg | CARBOHYDRATES: 56g | FIBER: 11g | SUGAR: 27g | PROTEIN: 31g

9

Desserts

One of the most delicious kinds of comfort food is desserts! In this chapter, you will learn how to make some traditionally deep-fried recipes in your air fryer along with shortcuts for making baked goods that come out extra crispy and delicious. There are plenty of dessert types for any comfort food fan: from fruit lovers to chocolate lovers and more. Fruit lovers will savor the Bananas Foster, Apple Pie Bombs, and "Grilled" Peaches. Chocolate lovers will adore the Chocolate Cake Donuts, Chocolate Chip Cookie Skillet, and Chewy Chocolate Chip Brownies. Not into fruit or chocolate? Try the Beignets, Coconut Macaroons, Powdered Donuts, or Pecan Sandies. There is a dessert for everyone in this delicious dessert chapter.

Donut Holes

You no longer have to go to your favorite fast-food bakery chain to get some delicious donut holes. You can make them quickly and easily in the air fryer. This no-yeast recipe comes out sweet and chewy. These Donut Holes are best enjoyed the same day they're made but can be stored in an airtight container at room temperature for up to 3 days. Pair them with a glass of milk or a cup of coffee.

Hands-On Time: 20 minutes
Cook Time: 8 minutes (per batch)

Serves 4

2 cups all-purpose flour
1 cup granulated sugar
1½ tablespoons baking powder
½ teaspoon salt
¼ teaspoon ground nutmeg
1 cup whole milk
1 large egg
1 teaspoon vanilla extract
½ cup unsalted melted butter, divided
1 cup confectioners' sugar

1 Preheat air fryer to 375°F.

2 In a large bowl, combine flour, granulated sugar, baking powder, salt, and nutmeg. Mix until combined. In a small bowl, mix together milk, egg, and vanilla. Make a well in the flour mixture and pour in wet ingredients from small bowl. Fold until just combined. Pour in ¼ cup melted butter and stir until combined. Scoop heaping tablespoons of dough and roll into 1½" balls.

3 Spray inside of air fryer with olive oil spray. Arrange holes inside air fryer in a single layer, spaced ½" apart. Air fry 8 minutes or until golden brown. Work in batches if needed, spraying inside of air fryer with olive oil spray each time.

4 Remove holes from air fryer. While still hot, dip in remaining ¼ cup melted butter and then in confectioners' sugar. Serve.

PER SERVING

CALORIES: 782 | FAT: 25g | SODIUM: 888mg | CARBOHYDRATES: 127g | FIBER: 2g | SUGAR: 78g | PROTEIN: 10g

Chewy Chocolate Chip Brownies

Decadent chewy brownies filled with chocolate chips baked in the air fryer? The result is a pan of warm, chocolaty brownies! They're perfect on their own but even better with a scoop of vanilla ice cream. For a fudgier consistency, place cooled brownies in the refrigerator for 1 hour prior to serving.

Hands-On Time: 15 minutes
Cook Time: 15 minutes

Serves 4

½ cup all-purpose flour
6 tablespoons unsweetened cocoa powder
¾ cup granulated sugar
¼ cup plus 1 tablespoon unsalted butter, melted
2 large eggs
½ teaspoon vanilla extract
¼ teaspoon salt
¼ teaspoon baking powder
1 cup semisweet chocolate chips, divided

1 Preheat air fryer to 330°F. Spray a 7" cake pan with olive oil spray and set aside.

2 In a large bowl, combine flour, cocoa powder, sugar, butter, eggs, vanilla, salt, and baking powder. Mix until just combined but still lumpy. Fold in ½ cup chocolate chips.

3 Pour batter in prepared cake pan.

4 Place pan inside air fryer and air fry 13 minutes. Top brownies with remaining ½ cup chocolate chips and air fry 2 more minutes.

5 Remove pan from air fryer and transfer to a cooling rack to cool 30 minutes. Serve.

PER SERVING

CALORIES: 602 | FAT: 30g | SODIUM: 219mg | CARBOHYDRATES: 84g | FIBER: 6g | SUGAR: 63g | PROTEIN: 8g

Chocolate Chip Cookie Skillet

These cookie skillets are very popular in restaurants, and for a good reason. They're deliciously sweet! Good news: You can easily re-create this delicious dessert at home in your air fryer. You will need a 7" cake pan or pie plate and the basic ingredients for chocolate chip cookies.

Hands-On Time: 15 minutes
Cook Time: 10 minutes

Serves 4

1 cup plus 2 tablespoons all-purpose flour
½ teaspoon baking soda
½ teaspoon salt
6 tablespoons unsalted butter, softened
⅓ cup granulated sugar
¼ cup packed light brown sugar
1 large egg
½ teaspoon vanilla extract
1 cup semisweet chocolate chips
½ cup vanilla ice cream

1 Preheat air fryer to 320°F. Spray a 7" cake pan with olive oil spray and set aside.

2 Combine flour, baking soda, and salt in a large bowl. In a second large bowl, using an electric mixer on medium speed, cream together butter, granulated sugar, and brown sugar. Mix in egg and vanilla. Make a well in dry ingredients and pour wet ingredients into the center. Mix with electric mixer, an additional 1 minute or until combined. Fold in chocolate chips.

3 Pour cookie batter into prepared cake pan. Place cake pan inside air fryer and air fry 10 minutes or until a toothpick inserted in the center comes out clean.

4 Remove from air fryer. Serve with vanilla ice cream.

PER SERVING

CALORIES: 669 | FAT: 32g | SODIUM: 490mg | CARBOHYDRATES: 90g | FIBER: 4g | SUGAR: 59g | PROTEIN: 8g

S'mores

This recipe reflects the classic version of s'mores, but you can replace the chocolate with your favorite chocolate candy bar.

Hands-On Time: 5 minutes
Cook Time: 5 minutes

Serves 4

4 graham crackers, halved
2 marshmallows, halved
2 (1.55-ounce) milk chocolate candy bars, halved

1 Preheat air fryer to 390°F.

2 Arrange 4 graham cracker halves inside air fryer in a single layer. Top each graham cracker half with a marshmallow half (sticky side down). Air fry 5 minutes or until marshmallows are golden brown.

3 Working quickly, carefully remove graham crackers and marshmallows from air fryer. Top each marshmallow with a chocolate bar half and a graham cracker half. Press graham cracker halves together and serve.

PER SERVING

CALORIES: 188 | FAT: 7g | SODIUM: 84mg | CARBOHYDRATES: 27g | FIBER: 1g | SUGAR: 17g | PROTEIN: 3g

"Grilled" Peaches

Peaches "grilled" in the air fryer come out juicy and sweet with a crunchy, caramelized skin. Serve them on top of some vanilla ice cream for a nice hot-and-cold sweet dessert.

Hands-On Time: 15 minutes
Cook Time: 10 minutes

Serves 4

4 medium peaches, halved and pitted
2 tablespoons olive oil
½ cup unsalted butter, softened
2 tablespoons granulated sugar
1 teaspoon cinnamon sugar
¼ teaspoon salt

1 Preheat air fryer to 350°F.

2 Brush both sides of peaches with olive oil. Place peaches (skin side down) inside air fryer.

3 Air fry 5 minutes. Flip peaches over and air fry an additional 5 minutes.

4 In a small bowl, mx together butter, granulated sugar, cinnamon sugar, and salt.

5 Remove peaches from air fryer and spread them with cinnamon butter. Serve.

PER SERVING

CALORIES: 349 | FAT: 28g | SODIUM: 148mg | CARBOHYDRATES: 21g | FIBER: 2g | SUGAR: 20g | PROTEIN: 2g

Apple Pie

Make this classic pie in your air fryer and avoid heating up your whole house. It's delicious and quick—especially compared to an oven-baked pie. For this recipe, you will need a 7" pie pan, which is slightly smaller than the traditional size. If you don't have one, a 7" cake pan can be used.

Hands-On Time: 15 minutes
Cook Time: 20 minutes

Serves 4

- 1 (15-ounce) package refrigerated premade pie crust dough containing 2 crusts
- 4 medium Granny Smith apples, peeled, cored, and thinly sliced
- ½ cup sugar
- 1½ tablespoons all-purpose flour
- 1 tablespoon lemon juice
- ¾ teaspoon ground cinnamon
- ¼ teaspoon salt
- ⅛ teaspoon ground nutmeg
- 1 large egg white
- 1 tablespoon water
- 1 tablespoon cinnamon sugar

1 Preheat air fryer to 320°F. Spray a 7" pie pan with olive oil spray.

2 Unroll pie crusts. Gently press 1 pie crust into prepared pie pan and set aside.

3 In a medium bowl, mix together apples, sugar, flour, lemon juice, cinnamon, salt, and nutmeg. Pour apple pie filling into pie pan and top with second pie crust. Gently crimp the edges of the pie crusts and cut three (2") slits in the center of the top pie crust.

4 In a small bowl, mix together egg white and water. Use a pastry brush to coat top pie crust with egg wash.

5 Gently place pie pan inside air fryer. Air fry 20 minutes or until top crust is golden brown.

6 Remove pie pan from air fryer. Sprinkle pie with cinnamon sugar. Let cool 2 hours and serve.

PER SERVING

CALORIES: 635 | FAT: 24g | SODIUM: 710mg | CARBOHYDRATES: 102g | FIBER: 2g | SUGAR: 44g | PROTEIN: 3g

Red Velvet Cake

Light and fluffy chocolate cake topped with a slightly sweet cream cheese frosting, this Red Velvet Cake is fancy enough for a birthday or other important event, yet easy enough to make for an ordinary Sunday dinner at home. Go as intricate with decorations as you would like, or keep it simple and rustic.

Hands-On Time: 20 minutes
Cook Time: 20 minutes

Serves 6

- 1¼ cups cake flour
- ¾ teaspoon unsweetened cocoa powder
- ¾ teaspoon salt, divided
- ½ cup buttermilk
- 1 teaspoon vanilla extract, divided
- ½ teaspoon baking soda
- 1 large egg
- ¾ teaspoon white vinegar
- 1 cup unsalted butter plus 2 tablespoons, softened and divided
- 1 cup granulated sugar
- 10 drops red food coloring
- 4 ounces cream cheese, softened
- 2 cups confectioners' sugar

1 Preheat air fryer to 320°F. Spray a 7" cake pan with olive oil spray and set aside.

2 In a large bowl, mix together flour, cocoa powder, and ½ teaspoon salt. Set aside. In a medium bowl, mix together buttermilk, ½ teaspoon vanilla, baking soda, and egg. Mix in vinegar. Set aside. In another large bowl, cream together 1 cup butter and granulated sugar.

3 Slowly add flour mixture and buttermilk mixture to butter mixture. Mix until fully combined. Pour in food coloring and stir until batter is evenly dyed red.

4 Pour batter into prepared cake pan and place inside air fryer. Air fry 20 minutes or until a toothpick inserted in the center of the cake comes out clean. Remove from air fryer and let cool 2 hours.

5 In a medium bowl, cream together cream cheese, remaining 2 tablespoons butter, remaining ½ teaspoon vanilla, and remaining ¼ teaspoon salt. Slowly mix in confectioners' sugar until smooth.

6 Frost cake with cream cheese frosting and serve.

PER SERVING

CALORIES: 768 | FAT: 39g | SODIUM: 503mg | CARBOHYDRATES: 91g | FIBER: 1g | SUGAR: 68g | PROTEIN: 6g

Beignets

Beignets are a donut-type pastry that are traditionally deep-fried and then coated in confectioners' sugar. This recipe teaches you how to cook the tasty treat in your air fryer in just 14 minutes.

Hands-On Time: 30 minutes
Cook Time: 14 minutes (per batch)

Serves 8

3¼ cups all-purpose flour, divided
¾ teaspoon salt
3 tablespoons granulated sugar, divided
1 cup whole milk, warm
2 teaspoons active dry yeast
1 large egg
3 tablespoons unsalted butter, melted
3 cups confectioners' sugar

1 In a large bowl, mix together 3 cups flour, salt, and 2 tablespoons granulated sugar.

2 In a small bowl, mix together warm milk, remaining 1 tablespoon granulated sugar, and yeast. Let sit 10 minutes or until foamy.

3 Mix egg into yeast mixture. Pour the wet ingredients into the bowl of dry ingredients. Mix until a soft dough forms, about 2 minutes. Slowly pour in melted butter and continue to mix until fully incorporated. Sprinkle remaining ¼ cup flour onto a clean surface. Place dough on floured surface. Knead until smooth and no longer sticky, adding more flour if needed, about 5 minutes. Shape dough into a ball and place inside a medium bowl sprayed with olive oil spray. Place bowl in a warm spot in your kitchen, cover loosely with a clean towel, and let rise until doubled in size, about 1 hour.

4 Preheat air fryer to 350°F. Spray inside of air fryer with olive oil spray.

5 Roll dough into a log shape, approximately 10" 14". Cut dough into sixteen equal pieces.

6 Arrange dough inside air fryer, spaced ½" apart (you may need to work in batches). Air fry 14 minutes, flipping halfway through.

7 Remove beignets from air fryer, dip in confectioners' sugar, and serve.

PER SERVING

CALORIES: 344 | **FAT:** 6g | **SODIUM:** 242mg | **CARBOHYDRATES:** 64g | **FIBER:** 2g | **SUGAR:** 25g | **PROTEIN:** 7g

Chocolate Cake Donuts

These sweet chocolate donuts are air fried until perfectly cooked and then dipped in a glaze of confectioners' sugar and milk. What a great comfort food! This recipe does require a donut pan that will fit inside your air fryer. There are several donut pans specifically made for the air fryer that should work. If you cannot find a donut pan to fit your air fryer, a silicone pan may be used and cut down to size.

Hands-On Time: 20 minutes
Cook Time: 5 minutes

Serves 5 (2 each)

1 cup all-purpose flour
½ cup granulated sugar
¼ cup unsweetened cocoa powder
¼ cup semisweet mini chocolate chips
½ teaspoon baking soda
¼ teaspoon salt
1 large egg
6 tablespoons sour cream
½ cup whole milk, divided
¼ cup vegetable oil
1½ teaspoons vanilla extract, divided
1½ cups confectioners' sugar

1 Preheat air fryer to 350°F. Spray a small donut pan with olive oil spray and set aside.

2 In a large bowl, combine flour, granulated sugar, cocoa powder, chocolate chips, baking soda, and salt. In a medium bowl, mix together egg, sour cream, ¼ cup milk, vegetable oil, and ½ teaspoon vanilla. Mix wet ingredients into dry ingredients. Stir until just combined but still lumpy.

3 Spoon donut batter into prepared donut pan. Carefully place pan inside air fryer. Air fry 5 minutes. Remove from air fryer.

4 In a small bowl, mix together remaining ¼ cup milk, remaining 1 teaspoon vanilla, and confectioners' sugar until smooth. Dip each cooked donut in glaze and transfer to a wire rack to cool and set, about 10 minutes. Serve.

PER SERVING

CALORIES: 498 | FAT: 18g | SODIUM: 281mg | CARBOHYDRATES: 78g | FIBER: 3g | SUGAR: 56g | PROTEIN: 6g

Chocolate Chip Bread Pudding

This delicious custard dessert is made with leftover French bread that absorbs the flavors of vanilla extract and heavy cream and turns it into a creamy bread pudding. If working with fresh bread, cube the bread and toast in the air fryer at 350°F for 3–4 minutes.

Hands-On Time: 15 minutes
Cook Time: 15 minutes

Serves 6

2 cups cubed stale French bread
¼ cup semisweet mini chocolate chips
⅔ cup heavy cream
¼ cup granulated sugar
1 large egg
½ teaspoon vanilla extract

1 Preheat air fryer to 350°F. Spray a 7" cake pan with olive oil spray.

2 Arrange bread cubes in an even layer in prepared cake pan. Top with mini chocolate chips.

3 In a medium bowl, mix together heavy cream, sugar, egg, and vanilla. Pour cream mixture over bread in cake pan. Let sit 5 minutes.

4 Place cake pan inside air fryer and air fry 15 minutes.

5 Remove from air fryer and serve.

PER SERVING

CALORIES: 222 | FAT: 12g | SODIUM: 136mg | CARBOHYDRATES: 24g | FIBER: 1g | SUGAR: 14g | PROTEIN: 4g

Baked Apples

These sweet apples are filled with cinnamon, pecans, and brown sugar and air fried until tender. They're like a nutty, sweet apple pie filling. Serve them with a scoop of vanilla ice cream to enhance the warm and sugary baked apple flavor. This recipe calls for Golden Delicious apples, but Gala, Honeycrisp, or Granny Smith apples may be used.

Hands-On Time: 20 minutes
Cook Time: 20 minutes

Serves 4

4 Golden Delicious apples
¼ cup packed light brown sugar
¼ cup chopped pecans
¼ cup raisins
1 teaspoon ground cinnamon
4 teaspoons unsalted butter

1 Preheat air fryer to 350°F.

2 Carefully core each apple, leaving the bottom ½" of each apple intact.

3 In a medium bowl, combine brown sugar, pecans, raisins, and cinnamon. Spoon mixture into the center of each apple and top with 1 teaspoon butter.

4 Carefully place apples inside air fryer. Air fry 20 minutes.

5 Remove from air fryer and serve.

PER SERVING

CALORIES: 261 | FAT: 8g | SODIUM: 8mg | CARBOHYDRATES: 46g | FIBER: 5g | SUGAR: 37g | PROTEIN: 2g

Cannoli

This recipe includes directions for making homemade cannoli shells in the air fryer before filling them with the sweet cream filling. The most time-consuming step of making cannoli is draining the ricotta. It needs to drain for a minimum of 12 hours prior to preparing this recipe.

Hands-On Time: 30 minutes
Cook Time: 5 minutes

Serves 12

- 2 cups all-purpose flour, divided
- 2 tablespoons granulated sugar
- ½ teaspoon salt
- 3 tablespoons unsalted butter, cut into small cubes
- 1 large egg
- ⅓ cup marsala wine
- 1 (32-ounce) container whole milk ricotta, strained overnight
- 1½ cups confectioners' sugar
- ¼ teaspoon ground cinnamon
- 1 cup heavy whipping cream
- ¾ cup semisweet mini chocolate chips

HOW TO DRAIN RICOTTA

Line a strainer with cheesecloth and place it over a large bowl. Place the ricotta over the cheesecloth and cover with another piece of cheesecloth. Place something heavy on top and refrigerate overnight.

1 Combine 1¾ cups flour, granulated sugar, and salt in a large bowl and mix. Mix in butter using fork until pea-sized lumps form. Mix in egg and marsala wine. Continue to stir until a rough dough forms. Remove dough from bowl and knead until smooth and no longer sticky, about 4 minutes. Wrap dough in plastic wrap and let rest 2 hours at room temperature.

2 Preheat air fryer to 400°F. Spray inside of air fryer with olive oil spray.

3 Sprinkle remaining ¼ cup flour onto a clean surface. Roll out dough on the floured surface until ⅛" thick. Cut dough into 4" rounds and wrap each piece around a metal cannoli mold. Dip finger into a bit of water and seal the edge of the dough with water. Carefully place cannoli dough in air fryer, spaced ½" apart. Spray with olive oil spray and air fry 5 minutes. Remove from air fryer and let cool completely, about 15 minutes.

4 In a large bowl, mix together ricotta, confectioners' sugar, and cinnamon. Set aside. Whisk whipping cream until stiff peaks form, about 5 minutes with an electric mixer or 10 minutes by hand. Fold ricotta mixture into whipped cream. Refrigerate until ready to use.

5 Fill a pastry bag with ricotta mixture and pipe inside each cannoli shell. Dip each end of cannoli into mini chocolate chips. Serve.

PER SERVING

CALORIES: 519 | **FAT:** 22g | **SODIUM:** 190mg | **CARBOHYDRATES:** 66g | **FIBER:** 1g | **SUGAR:** 48g | **PROTEIN:** 12g

Monkey Bread

This Monkey Bread transforms store-bought biscuit dough balls into a buttery cinnamon sugar dessert. It's a surefire easy dessert that will have people coming back for seconds. Serve by having your guests pull off pieces of the bread one by one to eat.

Hands-On Time: 15 minutes
Cook Time: 25 minutes

Serves 6

1 (16.3-ounce) can refrigerated biscuit dough
3 tablespoons cinnamon
1 cup granulated sugar
½ cup packed light brown sugar
½ cup unsalted butter, melted
½ cup confectioners' sugar
1 teaspoon whole milk
½ teaspoon vanilla extract

WHY IS IT CALLED MONKEY BREAD?

Monkey bread got its name because it is eaten by picking off the little balls of cooked dough one by one—similar to the way monkeys groom each other.

1 Preheat air fryer to 350°F. Grease a small Bundt pan and set aside.

2 Remove biscuit dough from tube and cut into 1" pieces. Combine cinnamon and granulated sugar in a gallon-sized zip-top bag. Add in biscuit dough and seal the bag. Shake to evenly coat dough. Arrange dough evenly in prepared Bundt pan.

3 Mix together brown sugar and butter in a small bowl. Pour over biscuit dough. Place Bundt pan into air fryer. Air fry 25 minutes.

4 In a medium bowl, mix together confectioners' sugar, milk, and vanilla.

5 Remove pan from air fryer. Let monkey bread cool on a cooling rack 15 minutes. Pour glaze over monkey bread and serve.

PER SERVING

CALORIES: 613 | **FAT:** 22g | **SODIUM:** 760mg | **CARBOHYDRATES:** 99g | **FIBER:** 3g | **SUGAR:** 65g | **PROTEIN:** 5g

Coconut Macaroons

These tasty desserts are made with a combination of sweetened shredded coconut and sweetened condensed milk. They come out light and crispy. Macaroons can be stored in an airtight container at room temperature for up to 3 days.

Hands-On Time: 15 minutes
Cook Time: 5 minutes (per batch)

Serves 10

1 (14-ounce) package sweetened shredded coconut
1 (14-ounce) can sweetened condensed milk
1 teaspoon vanilla extract
2 large egg whites
¼ teaspoon salt

CHOCOLATE-DIPPED MACAROONS

Melt a 14-ounce semisweet chocolate bar. Dip the bottom of each macaroon in the chocolate. Transfer to parchment paper, chocolate side down, to cool and set.

1 Preheat air fryer to 320°F.

2 Combine coconut, condensed milk, and vanilla in a large bowl. Mix until evenly coated. In a medium bowl, whisk egg whites and salt until stiff peaks form, about 5 minutes with an electric mixer or 10 minutes by hand. Gently fold egg whites into the coconut mixture, just until combined.

3 Spray inside of air fryer with olive oil spray before each batch. Scoop heaping tablespoons of batter and place inside air fryer, spaced ½" apart (you may need to work in batches). Air fry 5 minutes or until golden brown.

4 Remove from air fryer. Let cool 10 minutes and serve.

PER SERVING

CALORIES: 312 | **FAT:** 14g | **SODIUM:** 232mg | **CARBOHYDRATES:** 42g | **FIBER:** 4g | **SUGAR:** 36g | **PROTEIN:** 5g

Powdered Donuts

These delicious donuts come out perfectly cakey, and crisp on the outside. They are coated in confectioners' sugar fresh from the air fryer. Let them cool slightly before eating. This recipe does require a donut pan that will fit inside your air fryer. There are several donut pans specifically made for the air fryer that should work. If you cannot find a donut pan to fit your air fryer, a silicone pan may be used and cut down to size.

Hands-On Time: 20 minutes
Cook Time: 5 minutes (per batch)

Serves 12 (2 each)

2 cups all-purpose flour
¾ cup granulated sugar
2 teaspoons baking powder
½ teaspoon ground cinnamon
½ teaspoon salt
¼ teaspoon ground nutmeg
¾ cup buttermilk
2 large eggs
2 tablespoons vegetable oil
1 cup confectioners' sugar

1 Preheat air fryer to 350°F. Spray a donut pan with olive oil spray and set aside.

2 In a large bowl, combine flour, sugar, baking powder, cinnamon, salt, and nutmeg. Mix. In a medium bowl, mix together buttermilk, eggs, and vegetable oil. Add wet ingredients to dry ingredients and stir until just combined and still lumpy.

3 Spoon donut batter into prepared donut pan. Working in batches, air fry 5 minutes. Remove from air fryer, dip in confectioners' sugar, and place on a cooling rack to cool 15 minutes. Repeat with remaining donut batter. Serve.

PER SERVING

CALORIES: 199 | FAT: 4g | SODIUM: 206mg | CARBOHYDRATES: 38g | FIBER: 1g | SUGAR: 21g | PROTEIN: 4g

Oatmeal Raisin Cookies

These cookies come out perfectly chewy with just the right amount of sweetness from the raisins and sugar. The air fryer cooks them quickly and makes them extra crispy around the edges. The dough for these cookies can be made a day in advance and stored in the refrigerator.

Hands-On Time: 10 minutes
Cook Time: 5 minutes (per batch)

Serves 4 (2 each)

1 cup all-purpose flour
½ teaspoon salt
½ teaspoon baking powder
½ teaspoon ground cinnamon
¼ teaspoon baking soda
1 cup granulated sugar
½ cup unsalted butter, softened
1 teaspoon vanilla
2 large eggs
1½ cups old-fashioned rolled oats
1 cup raisins

1 Preheat air fryer to 340°F.

2 In a large bowl, combine flour, salt, baking powder, cinnamon, and baking soda. In a medium bowl, using an electric mixer on medium speed, cream together sugar and butter. Mix in vanilla and eggs and stir until combined. Make a well in dry ingredients and pour in wet ingredients. Mix until just combined. Fold in oats and raisins.

3 Spray inside of air fryer with olive oil spray before each batch. Place heaping tablespoons of cookie dough inside air fryer, spaced ½" apart (you may need to work in batches).

4 Air fry 5 minutes or until golden brown around the edges. Remove cookies and cool on a wire rack 10 minutes. Serve.

PER SERVING

CALORIES: 786 | FAT: 26g | SODIUM: 473mg | CARBOHYDRATES: 128g | FIBER: 6g | SUGAR: 75g | PROTEIN: 12g

Apple Pie Bombs

These Apple Pie Bombs are made of a buttery pastry dough with a surprise center of tender diced apples. No one will be expecting the surprise center! Serve them with a scoop of ice cream, or with a glass of milk to help balance the sweetness.

Hands-On Time: 10 minutes
Cook Time: 14 minutes (per batch)

Serves 8 (2 each)

¼ cup granulated sugar
½ teaspoon ground cinnamon
2 large Granny Smith apples, peeled, cored, and diced
1 teaspoon lemon juice
1 (16-ounce) can refrigerated biscuit dough
½ cup unsalted butter, melted

WHY ARE THEY CALLED BOMBS?

These delectable desserts are called Apple Pie Bombs because they burst like a bomb in your mouth. They will explode with flavor once they hit your taste buds.

1 Preheat air fryer to 325°F.

2 In a small bowl, add sugar and cinnamon. Mix until well combined. Place apples in a medium bowl and top with lemon juice and 1 tablespoon cinnamon sugar mixture. Stir until evenly coated. Reserve remaining cinnamon sugar.

3 Open biscuit package and divide each biscuit into two pieces. Roll each piece into a circle about 5" wide. Scoop 1 tablespoon apples into the center of each biscuit piece. Press the edges of the biscuit around the apples until sealed.

4 Spray inside of air fryer with olive oil spray before each batch. Arrange pie bombs in air fryer, spaced ½" apart, seam side down. Air fry 14 minutes, flipping halfway through (you may need to work in batches).

5 Remove pie bombs from air fryer. Dip into melted butter and then roll in remaining cinnamon sugar mixture. Serve.

PER SERVING

CALORIES: 326 | FAT: 16g | SODIUM: 555mg | CARBOHYDRATES: 40g | FIBER: 1g | SUGAR: 16g | PROTEIN: 4g

Pecan Sandies

Pecan Sandies are buttery shortbread cookies made with roasted pecans. They are delicious served with tea or coffee. This is a simple four-ingredient recipe made of butter, flour, brown sugar, and pecans. The dough log can be refrigerated up to 3 days or frozen up to 1 month.

Hands-On Time: 15 minutes
Cook Time: 5 minutes (per batch)

Serves 5 (3 each)

- ½ cup salted butter, cubed and chilled
- ¼ cup packed light brown sugar
- 1 cup all-purpose flour, divided
- ¼ cup finely chopped roasted pecans

THE NAME "SANDIES"

It may seem silly, but these tasty cookies are called "sandies" because their color resembles sand. That's where the inspiration ends—these cookies are not gritty at all!

1 In a large bowl, using an electric mixer on medium speed, combine butter and brown sugar and mix until creamy. Slowly mix in ¾ cup flour until combined. Fold in pecans.

2 Sprinkle remaining ¼ cup flour onto a clean surface and then place dough on surface. Knead dough 2 minutes or until no longer sticky. Roll dough into a 1½" log and wrap in plastic wrap. Refrigerate 1 hour.

3 Preheat air fryer to 320°F.

4 Remove dough from plastic wrap and slice into ½" thick rounds. Spray inside of air fryer with olive oil spray before each batch. Working in batches, place dough inside air fryer, spaced ½" apart. Air fry 5 minutes or until edges are golden brown.

5 Remove from air fryer and serve.

PER SERVING

CALORIES: 333 | FAT: 21g | SODIUM: 5mg | CARBOHYDRATES: 31g | FIBER: 1g | SUGAR: 11g | PROTEIN: 3g

Bananas Foster

Bananas Foster is a dessert made of sliced bananas covered in a rum sauce and served over vanilla ice cream. The bananas get perfectly caramelized in the air fryer while the sauce cooks and thickens. For a twist on a breakfast favorite, serve these Bananas Foster (with or without ice cream) on top of some pancakes or a Belgian waffle. Yum!

Hands-On Time: 15 minutes
Cook Time: 10 minutes

Serves 2

2 large bananas
⅔ cup plus 1 teaspoon packed light brown sugar, divided
¾ teaspoon ground cinnamon, divided
¼ cup unsalted butter
3 tablespoons rum
1 teaspoon vanilla extract
1 cup vanilla ice cream

BANANAS FOSTER ORIGIN
Bananas Foster originated at a restaurant called Brennan's Restaurant in Louisiana. This traditional restaurant has been serving New Orleans since 1946.

1   Preheat air fryer to 400°F.

2   Slice bananas in half lengthwise, leaving peel intact. Place banana halves inside air fryer, peel side down. Sprinkle banana halves with 1 teaspoon brown sugar and ¼ teaspoon ground cinnamon. Air fry 6 minutes. Remove from air fryer.

3   Melt butter in a small saucepan over medium heat. Mix in remaining ⅔ cup brown sugar, rum, vanilla, and remaining ½ teaspoon cinnamon. Let simmer 2 minutes.

4   Remove peels from bananas and pour sauce on top. Serve topped with vanilla ice cream.

PER SERVING

CALORIES: 787 | FAT: 28g | SODIUM: 77mg | CARBOHYDRATES: 122g | FIBER: 5g | SUGAR: 104g | PROTEIN: 4g

Caramel Apple Crisp

Use fresh, in-season apples to make this delicious crisp. This version uses tart Granny Smith apples coated in a cinnamon sugar mixture and topped with a crisp made of chewy oats sweetened with brown sugar. Serving the tender apples and crunchy oats with a scoop of vanilla ice cream is perfection.

Hands-On Time: 20 minutes
Cook Time: 25 minutes

Serves 4

3 large Granny Smith apples, peeled, cored, and thinly sliced
¼ cup granulated sugar
1 tablespoon lemon juice
1 teaspoon cinnamon
½ cup old-fashioned rolled oats
⅓ cup packed light brown sugar
¼ teaspoon salt
⅓ cup unsalted butter, melted
½ (14-ounce) package caramels, unwrapped
⅓ cup evaporated milk
1 cup vanilla ice cream

1 Preheat air fryer to 350°F. Spray a 7" cake pan with olive oil spray and set aside.

2 Toss apples, granulated sugar, lemon juice, and cinnamon in a medium bowl until evenly coated. Pour apples into sprayed cake pan.

3 In a second medium bowl, mix together oats, brown sugar, and salt. Pour in butter and stir until evenly coated. Pour oat mixture over apples.

4 In a small saucepan over low heat, heat caramels and evaporated milk. Stir constantly until caramels are melted and smooth. Pour caramel sauce over apple crisp.

5 Place prepared apple crisp in air fryer. Air fry 20 minutes. Remove from air fryer and let cool 10 minutes. Serve topped with vanilla ice cream.

PER SERVING

CALORIES: 656 | FAT: 24g | SODIUM: 322mg | CARBOHYDRATES: 107g | FIBER: 4g | SUGAR: 86g | PROTEIN: 7g

Small Batch Chocolate Chip Cookies

Do you want warm baked chocolate chip cookies, but don't want to make three dozen cookies or heat your whole house? This recipe gives you a small batch of warm, soft chocolate chip cookies that bake quickly in your air fryer. Dip them in milk.

Hands-On Time: 10 minutes
Cook Time: 8 minutes

Serves 3 (2 each)

- ⅔ cup all-purpose flour
- ¼ teaspoon baking soda
- ¼ teaspoon salt
- 4 tablespoons unsalted butter, softened
- ⅓ cup granulated sugar
- 2 tablespoons packed light brown sugar
- 1 large egg yolk
- 1 teaspoon vanilla extract
- ⅓ cup semisweet chocolate chips

1 Preheat air fryer to 350°F.

2 In a large bowl, mix together flour, baking soda, and salt. Set aside. In a second large bowl, using an electric mixer on medium speed, cream together butter and sugar. Add in egg yolk and vanilla. Mix well.

3 Create a well in the dry mixture and pour the wet ingredients into the center of the well. Use electric mixer on medium speed to mix until combined and wet. Fold in chocolate chips. Form dough into six even balls.

4 Spray inside of air fryer with olive oil spray. Arrange cookies inside air fryer, spaced ½" apart.

5 Air fry 8 minutes or until golden brown on the edges. Remove cookies and let cool on a wire rack 10 minutes. Serve.

PER SERVING

CALORIES: 476 | **FAT:** 22g | **SODIUM:** 307mg | **CARBOHYDRATES:** 66g | **FIBER:** 2g | **SUGAR:** 42g | **PROTEIN:** 5g

Small Batch Sugar Cookies

Whip up these cookies in under 30 minutes! They are perfectly buttery and sweet with some cheerful rainbow sprinkles as decoration. These cookies taste delicious on their own as an easy sweet treat or for a simple dessert. If you want to dress them up more, you can also frost them once they've cooled completely.

Hands-On Time: 10 minutes
Cook Time: 10 minutes

Serves 3 (2 each)

- 4 tablespoons unsalted butter, melted
- ¼ cup granulated sugar
- 1 large egg yolk
- ½ teaspoon vanilla extract
- ½ cup plus 2 tablespoons all-purpose flour
- ¼ teaspoon baking soda
- ⅛ teaspoon salt
- 2 tablespoons rainbow sprinkles

EASY ICING

Want to add a little something extra to your sugar cookies? Mix together 1 cup confectioners' sugar, 3 tablespoons milk, and 1 teaspoon vanilla extract. Add in food coloring, if desired.

1 Preheat air fryer to 350°F.

2 In a medium bowl, mix together butter, sugar, egg yolk, and vanilla. Mix until well combined. Add in flour, baking soda, and salt. Stir until just combined. Fold in sprinkles. Divide cookie dough into six equal pieces. Roll each piece into a ball.

3 Spray inside of air fryer with olive oil spray. Arrange cookies inside air fryer, spaced ½" apart.

4 Air fry 10 minutes or until the edges start to crack. Let cool 10 minutes. Serve.

PER SERVING

CALORIES: 344 | FAT: 18g | SODIUM: 206mg | CARBOHYDRATES: 45g | FIBER: 1g | SUGAR: 25g | PROTEIN: 4g

US/Metric Conversion Chart

VOLUME CONVERSIONS

US Volume Measure	Metric Equivalent
⅛ teaspoon	0.5 milliliter
¼ teaspoon	1 milliliter
½ teaspoon	2 milliliters
1 teaspoon	5 milliliters
½ tablespoon	7 milliliters
1 tablespoon (3 teaspoons)	15 milliliters
2 tablespoons (1 fluid ounce)	30 milliliters
¼ cup (4 tablespoons)	60 milliliters
⅓ cup	90 milliliters
½ cup (4 fluid ounces)	125 milliliters
⅔ cup	160 milliliters
¾ cup (6 fluid ounces)	180 milliliters
1 cup (16 tablespoons)	250 milliliters
1 pint (2 cups)	500 milliliters
1 quart (4 cups)	1 liter (about)

WEIGHT CONVERSIONS

US Weight Measure	Metric Equivalent
½ ounce	15 grams
1 ounce	30 grams
2 ounces	60 grams
3 ounces	85 grams
¼ pound (4 ounces)	115 grams
½ pound (8 ounces)	225 grams
¾ pound (12 ounces)	340 grams
1 pound (16 ounces)	454 grams

OVEN TEMPERATURE CONVERSIONS

Degrees Fahrenheit	Degrees Celsius
200 degrees F	95 degrees C
250 degrees F	120 degrees C
275 degrees F	135 degrees C
300 degrees F	150 degrees C
325 degrees F	160 degrees C
350 degrees F	180 degrees C
375 degrees F	190 degrees C
400 degrees F	205 degrees C
425 degrees F	220 degrees C
450 degrees F	230 degrees C

BAKING PAN SIZES

American	Metric
8 x 1½ inch round baking pan	20 x 4 cm cake tin
9 x 1½ inch round baking pan	23 x 3.5 cm cake tin
11 x 7 x 1½ inch baking pan	28 x 18 x 4 cm baking tin
13 x 9 x 2 inch baking pan	30 x 20 x 5 cm baking tin
2 quart rectangular baking dish	30 x 20 x 3 cm baking tin
15 x 10 x 2 inch baking pan	30 x 25 x 2 cm baking tin (Swiss roll tin)
9 inch pie plate	22 x 4 or 23 x 4 cm pie plate
7 or 8 inch springform pan	18 or 20 cm springform or loose bottom cake tin
9 x 5 x 3 inch loaf pan	23 x 13 x 7 cm or 2 lb narrow loaf or pâté tin
1½ quart casserole	1.5 liter casserole
2 quart casserole	2 liter casserole

Index

About the Author

Aileen Clark is a recipe developer and food blogger at AileenCooks.com. She has been featured on *HuffPost*, *TODAY Parents*, and *Money Saving Mom*, and her recipes have been shared on *foodgawker*, *Parade* Community Table, and *Country Living*. She was recognized as one of the top parenting bloggers in Sacramento and has partnered with many major brands, including Nabisco, Better Than Bouillon, Red Baron, Ling Ling, Huggies, Fisher-Price, StarKist, and Macy's. Aileen's mission is to connect with other moms in a way that helps make their lives easier and more fun. She loves creating new recipes for the Instant Pot® and runs an Instant Pot® group on *Facebook* focused on troubleshooting recipes and helping new users find success with cooking in the Instant Pot®. Aileen lives in Northern California with her husband and four children.

Delicious Air Fryer Recipes As Easy As ONE, TWO, THREE

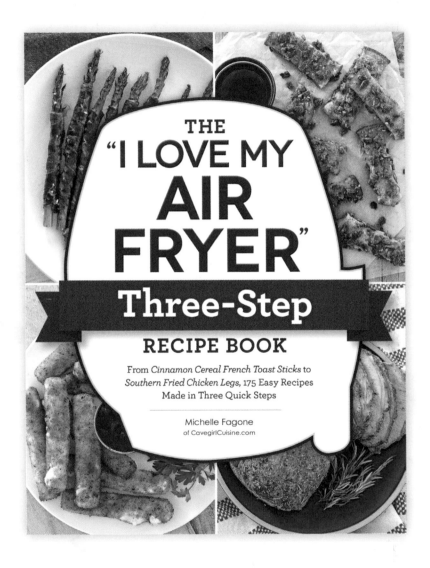

THE
"I LOVE MY
AIR
FRYER"
Three-Step
RECIPE BOOK

From *Cinnamon Cereal French Toast Sticks* to *Southern Fried Chicken Legs*, 175 Easy Recipes Made in Three Quick Steps

Michelle Fagone
of CavegirlCuisine.com

PICK UP OR DOWNLOAD YOUR COPY TODAY!

adamsmedia
An Imprint of Simon & Schuster
A Paramount Company